Cultivating Student Success

EMERGING ADULTHOOD SERIES

Series Editor
Larry J. Nelson

Advisory Board
Elisabetta Crocetti

Shagufa Kapadia

Koen Luyckx

Laura Padilla-Walker

Jennifer L. Tanner

Books in the Series
Emerging Adults' Religiousness and Spirituality: Meaning-Making in an Age of Transition
Edited by Carolyn M. Barry and Mona M. Abo-Zena

Flourishing in Emerging Adulthood: Positive Development During the
Third Decade of Life
Edited by Laura M. Padilla-Walker and Larry J. Nelson

The Marriage Paradox: Why Emerging Adults Love Marriage yet Push It Aside
Brian J. Willoughby and Spencer L. James

The Life Story, Domains of Identity, and Personality Development in Emerging
Adulthood: Integrating Narrative and Traditional Approaches
Michael W. Pratt and M. Kyle Matsuba

The Romantic Lives of Emerging Adults: Getting From I to We
Varda Konstam

Leaving Care and the Transition to Adulthood: International Contributions to Theory,
Research, and Practice
Edited by Varda Mann-Feder and Martin Goyette

Young Adult Development at the School-to-Work Transition:
International Pathways and Processes
Edited by E. Anne Marshall and Jennifer E. Symonds

The Experience of Emerging Adulthood Among Street-Involved Youth
Doug Magnuson, Mikael Jansson, and Cecilia Benoit

Sexuality in Emerging Adulthood
Edited by Elizabeth M. Morgan and Manfred H. M. van Dulmen

Generation Disaster: Coming of Age Post-9/11
Karla Vermeulen

Cultivating Student Success: A Multifaceted Approach to Working with Emerging Adults
in Higher Education
Edited by Tisha A. Duncan and Allison A. Buskirk-Cohen

Cultivating Student Success

A Multifaceted Approach to Working with Emerging Adults in Higher Education

Edited by

Tisha A. Duncan and Allison A. Buskirk-Cohen

OXFORD
UNIVERSITY PRESS

OXFORD
UNIVERSITY PRESS

Oxford University Press is a department of the University of Oxford. It furthers the University's objective of excellence in research, scholarship, and education by publishing worldwide. Oxford is a registered trade mark of Oxford University Press in the UK and certain other countries.

Published in the United States of America by Oxford University Press
198 Madison Avenue, New York, NY 10016, United States of America.

Library of Congress Cataloging-in-Publication Data
Names: Duncan, Tisha A., editor. | Buskirk-Cohen, Allison A., editor.
Title: Cultivating student success : a multifaceted approach to working with emerging adults in higher education / edited by Tisha A. Duncan and Allison A. Buskirk-Cohen.
Description: New York, NY : Oxford University Press, [2022] | Includes bibliographical references and index.
Identifiers: LCCN 2021031140 (print) | LCCN 2021031141 (ebook) | ISBN 9780197586693 (paperback) | ISBN 9780197586716 (epub) | ISBN 9780197586723 (digital online)
Subjects: LCSH: Counseling in higher education—United States. | College students—United States—Psychology. | Young adults—United States—Psychology. | Teacher-student relationships—United States. | Academic achievement—United States.
Classification: LCC LB2343 .C85 2021 (print) | LCC LB2343 (ebook) | DDC 378.1/9—dc23
LC record available at https://lccn.loc.gov/2021031140
LC ebook record available at https://lccn.loc.gov/2021031141

DOI: 10.1093/oso/9780197586693.001.0001

1 3 5 7 9 8 6 4 2

Printed by Marquis, Canada

Contents

Series Foreword   vii

Contributors   xi

Introduction—Not a Younger Version of You: How an Understanding of Emerging Adulthood Applies to Today's College Students   1

Tisha A. Duncan and Allison A. Buskirk-Cohen

1. "I Am _____": Self-Awareness, Self-Efficacy, and Self-Motivation in Emerging Adults   8

Joel A. Lane and Deanna N. Cor

2. "I Just Can't": Why are Emerging Adults Feeling More Anxious and Uncertain?   22

Alan Meca, Kelsie Allison, Julie Rodil, Kenneth L. Ayers, and Kyle Eichas

3. "We Got In!": The Influence and Role of Family on Relationships and Decision-Making   38

Kayla Reed-Fitzke and Elizabeth R. Watters

4. "I Took a Screenshot": Experiences with Technology In and Out of the Classroom   53

Joan A. Swanson and Allison A. Buskirk-Cohen

5. "^^ KWIM? BRB": How Do Emerging Adults Communicate Differently than Previous Generations?   68

Heather T. Rowan-Kenyon, Adam M. McCready, Ana M. Martínez Alemán, and Allison Yarri

6. "You're My Person": Building Meaningful Relationships with Emerging Adults   82

Thuha (Ha) Hoang and Lindsey (Ellen) Caillouet

7. "I've Never Had to Do This on My Own": Support to Address Retention and Success for Emerging Adults   95

Kevin Correa and Sylvia Symonds

8. "Guiding My Success": Providing a Developmental Lens to
   Strengthen the Whole Person   110
   Larry J. Nelson

Index   125

Series Foreword

The *Emerging Adulthood Series* examines the period of life starting at age 18 and continuing into and through the third decade of life, now commonly referred to as emerging adulthood. The specific focus of the series is on flourishing (i.e., factors that lead to positive, adaptive development during emerging adulthood and the successful transition into adult roles) and floundering (i.e., factors that lead to maladaptive behaviors and negative development during emerging adulthood as well as delay and difficulty in transitioning into adult roles) in the diverse paths young people take into and through the third decade of life.

There is a need to examine the successes and struggles in a variety of domains experienced by young people as they take complex and multiple paths in leaving adolescence and moving into and through their 20s. Too often the diversity of individual experiences is forgotten in our academic attempts to categorize a time period. For example, in proposing his theory of emerging adulthood, Arnett (2000, 2004) identified features of the development of young people including *feeling in-between* (emerging adults do not see themselves as either adolescents or adults), *identity exploration* (especially in the areas of work, love, and world views), *focus on the self* (not self-centered, but simply lacking obligations to others), *instability* (evidenced by changes of direction in residential status, relationships, work, and education), and *possibilities* (optimism in the potential to steer their lives in any number of desired directions). Although this is a nice summary of characteristics of the time period, the scholarly examination of emerging adulthood has not always attempted to capture and explain the within-group variation that exists among emerging adults, often making the broad generalization that they are a relatively homogenous group. For example, emerging adults have been categorically referred to as "narcissistic," "refusing to grow up," and "failed adults." While there certainly are emerging adults who fit the profile of selfish, struggling, and directionless, there are others who are using this period of time for good. Indeed, there is great diversity of individual experiences in emerging adulthood. Hence, there is a need to better examine various beliefs/attitudes, attributes, behaviors, and relationships during this period of time that appear to reflect positive adjustment, or a sense of flourishing, or conversely those that lead to floundering.

For example, recent research (Nelson & Padilla-Walker, 2013) shows that young people who appear to be successfully navigating emerging adulthood tend to engage in identity exploration, develop internalization of positive values, participate in positive media use, engage in prosocial behaviors, report healthy relationships with parents, and engage in romantic relationships that are characterized by higher levels of companionship, worth, affection, and emotional support. For others who appear to be floundering, emerging adulthood appears to include anxiety and depression, poor self-perceptions, greater participation in risky behaviors, and poorer relationship quality with parents, best friends, and romantic partners. Thus, while various profiles of flourishing and floundering are starting to be identified, the current work in the field has simply provided cursory overviews of findings. This series provides a platform for an in-depth, comprehensive examination into some of these key factors that seem to be influencing, positively or negatively, young people as they enter into and progress through the third decade of life and the multiple ways in which they may flourish or flounder. Furthermore, the series attempts to examine how these factors may function differently within various populations (i.e., cultures and religious and ethnic subcultures, students vs. nonstudents, men vs. women, etc.). Finally, the series provides for a multidisciplinary (e.g., fields including developmental psychology, neurobiology, education, sociology, and criminology) and multimethod (i.e., information garnered from both quantitative and qualitative methodologies) examination of issues related to flourishing and floundering in emerging adulthood.

It is important to make one final note about this series. In choosing to employ the term "emerging adulthood," it is not meant to imply that the series will include books that are limited in their scope to viewing the third decade of life only through the lens of emerging adulthood theory (Arnett, 2000). Indeed, the notion of "emerging adulthood" as a universal developmental period has been met with controversy and skepticism because of the complex and numerous paths young people take out of adolescence and into adulthood. It is that exact diversity in the experiences of young people in a variety of contexts and circumstances (e.g., cultural, financial, familial) that calls for a book series such as this one. It is unfortunate that disagreement about emerging adulthood theory has led to a fragmentation of scholars and scholarship devoted to better understanding the third decade of life. Hence, although the term "emerging adulthood" is employed for parsimony and for its growing familiarity as a term for the age period, this series is devoted to examining broadly the complexity of pathways into and through the third decade of life from a variety of perspectives and disciplines. In doing so, it is my hope that the series will help scholars, practitioners, students, and others better understand, and thereby potentially foster, flourishing and floundering in the lives of young people in the various paths they may take to adulthood.

Cultivating Student Success

It seems there is a growing disconnect between those who study the development of emerging adults and those who work with them in the context of higher education. On the one hand, scholars are attempting to understand the development of emerging adults generally (rather than in the context of higher education specifically), while many who work in the context of higher education (administrators, support services, faculty) tend to focus specifically on the ways to help students succeed academically without the perspective of emerging adult development more broadly. The result? There is often a failure to recognize the large number of emerging adults who might be served if there was a greater understanding of the role of development in their pursuit of higher education. In other words, if administrators, staff, and faculty believe that the role of higher education is to focus solely on conveying academic information, they are ignoring the evidence that students flourish when they are doing well in all areas of their lives. Indeed, research shows that students who perform best are prepared not only with the skills to succeed academically but also with the abilities to navigate the interpersonal and intrapersonal demands of university life. It is naïve to think that academic engagement can be separated from other important aspects of emerging adult development including psychological, interpersonal, and intrapersonal well-being. In sum, it is important to see and understand that all domains of development are interconnected and situated within the context of where emerging adults are in their development.

Because of this disconnect between understanding emerging adults' development broadly and their success in higher education specifically, the need for *Cultivating Student Success* cannot be overstated. Dr. Tisha Duncan and Dr. Allison Buskirk-Cohen have identified some of the most important aspects of emerging adulthood development to explicate how a better understanding of these topics can help those in higher education better serve students. The book focuses on how emerging adults are striving to understand their identity, balance mental health issues, and recenter relationships with parents, all while living minute to minute immersed in technology. It is within these developmental contexts and strivings that young people are trying to juggle the educational demands of being a student in settings of higher education. Again, to think that students can set aside their struggles of mental and emotional health to do homework is naïve. To think that picking a major is not part of a broader search for their identity is foolish. To think that strained relationships with parents do not affect performance on exams is misguided. *Cultivating Student Success* brilliantly describes how these key features of emerging adults' development must be understood to truly serve students in higher education. To demonstrate how understanding development can benefit members of the higher education community (administrators, service providers, faculty) in doing their jobs, the chapters include case studies, key questions, and practical recommendations for using the information. In sum, the book provides both a scholarly look into the development of emerging adults and a practical lens of how to use the information to foster student success in higher education.

Contributors

Kelsie Allison is a second-year student in the Health Psychology PhD program at Old Dominion University. She received her BA in Psychology from Christopher Newport University in 2018. Her research interests include promoting positive identity development for various populations (e.g., racial minorities, first-generation college students, college athletes) by examining identity processes and individual and contextual assets and how they relate to various outcomes such as mental health, academic achievement, and overall well-being.

Kenneth L. Ayers, MA, is a Clinical Psychology PhD student at the Virginia Consortium Program in Clinical Psychology, Norfolk, Virginia. He received his BS in Biology from Florida Agricultural and Mechanical University, Tallahassee, Florida, and MA in Psychology—Clinical Counseling from the Citadel, Charleston, South Carolina. His clinical interests include working with minoritized populations, veterans and military personnel and their families, and college students. His research focuses on the impact of discrimination, trauma, and psychosocial stressors on the functioning, well-being, and interpersonal relationships of minoritized and military/veteran populations, with a key focus on males (i.e., masculinity and gender roles).

Allison A. Buskirk-Cohen, PhD, is an educator, scholar, and leader in higher education with experience developing educational programs and resources aimed at supporting student success. Her research focuses on how interpersonal relationships influence well-being and has demonstrated how powerful the need to connect with others is, particularly within education. She also has served as editor of the textbook *Taking Sides: Clashing Views in Life-Span Development*.

Lindsey (Ellen) Caillouet, PhD, is an instructor in the Department of Teaching and Learning at Southeastern Louisiana University. Dr. Caillouet received her PhD in Educational Administration from the University of New Orleans, Louisiana. She studies educational leadership, elementary education, and emotional intelligence in K-12 and higher education. She teaches undergraduate courses in mathematics curriculum and instruction and a graduate course in educational statistics and research.

Deanna N. Cor, PhD, LPC, is an assistant professor and program coordinator in the Counselor Education Department at Portland State University. Dr. Cor's scholarship focuses on developing and enhancing multicultural and social justice counseling competencies in counseling students and current practitioners, specifically for working with clients identifying as trans and gender expansive. Her clinical specialty areas include working with LGBTQ individuals, exploring life transitions and relational concerns. Dr. Cor is the cofounder of the Oregon chapter of the Society for Sexual, Affectional, Intersex, and Gender Expansive Identities in counseling. She has published numerous peer-reviewed articles and book chapters and continues to engage in ongoing research to improve counselor education curriculum, training, and practitioner competency.

Kevin Correa, EdD, is the director of the Arizona State University (ASU) First-Year Success Center, which provides holistic and personalized peer success coaching to thousands of students each year. Nearly his entire career has been devoted to the engagement, retention, and success of diverse student populations at large public universities, and much of his work has been in leadership capacities. In addition to leading the First-Year Success Center, Dr. Correa serves as a faculty associate in ASU's Mary Lou Fulton Teachers College, where he teaches graduate-level courses in higher education.

Tisha A. Duncan, EdD, has extensive experience in coaching and supporting educators in the implementation of effective teaching practices in a variety of content areas. Her areas of specialty at both the undergraduate and graduate levels are curriculum and instruction, technology integration, and differentiation. Recent research interests include learner-centered instruction, collaboration, and emerging adulthood. With over 20 years in the field of education, she has been blessed with the opportunity to work with persons of diverse backgrounds and all ages, from birth through adulthood.

Kyle Eichas, PhD, is an associate professor in the Department of Psychological Sciences at Tarleton State University, Waco campus. He uses outreach research and community-engaged teaching to contribute to the evolution of effective and sustainable positive youth development interventions. Currently, his work is primarily focused on building collaborative projects in which college students work with community stakeholders to design, implement, and evaluate psychosocial intervention strategies for helping marginalized youth navigate the life course.

Thuha (Ha) Hoang, PhD is an assistant professor in the Department of Physical Therapy at the LSU Health Sciences Center, New Orleans. Dr. Hoang received her PhD in Curriculum and Instruction from the University of New Orleans, Louisiana. She studies student outcomes, academic success, program-based retention practices, and career development in higher and health professions education. She teaches graduate courses in the entry-level doctoral physical therapist program.

Joel A. Lane, PhD, LPC, is an associate professor and chair of the Counselor Education Department at Portland State University. His scholarly interests involve counseling considerations with emerging adult populations. Dr. Lane is the past president of the Oregon Counseling Association and is an active member of the Counseling and Counselor Education community locally and nationally.

Ana M. Martínez Alemán, EdD, is professor and associate dean for faculty and education at the Lynch School of Education and Human Development. Her recent books include *Critical Approaches to the Study of Higher Education* (Johns Hopkins University Press, 2015) and *Accountability, Pragmatic Aims, and the American University* (Routledge, 2011). She is coauthor of *Technology and Engagement: Making Technology Work for First Generation College Students* (Rutgers University Press, 2018) and *Online Social Networking on Campus: Understanding What Matters in Student Culture* (Routledge, 2009).

Adam M. McCready, PhD, is an assistant professor-in-residence of higher education and student affairs in the Neag School of Education Department of Educational Leadership at the University of Connecticut. His research examines the college student experience with the intent of identifying and challenging oppressive structures in higher education. He has studied the masculine norm climates of college social fraternities, college men and masculinities, and the encounters of students of color with racial hostilities on social media.

Alan Meca, PhD, is an assistant professor in the Department of Psychology at Old Dominion University but will transition to the Department of Psychology at University of Texas at San Antonio in fall 2021. His research program focuses on identity development across various domains and on the links between identity and psychosocial functioning. Dr. Meca serves on the Governing Council for the Society for the Study of Emerging Adulthood (SSEA) and has published over 70 peer-reviewed articles in leading journals in the field, including *Alcohol and Alcoholism*, *Cultural Diversity and Ethnic Minority Psychology*, *Developmental Psychology*, *Development and Psychopathology*, *Emerging Adulthood*, and *Journal of Youth and Adolescence*.

Larry J. Nelson, PhD, is professor in the School of Family Life at Brigham Young University. He studies factors that lead to flourishing and floundering in the transition to adulthood with particular interests in parenting, social withdrawal, identity, beliefs about adulthood, and culture. He has coedited a book entitled *Flourishing in Emerging Adulthood* published by Oxford University Press as part of this book series. He is president of the Society for the Study of Emerging Adulthood.

Kayla Reed-Fitzke, PhD, LMFT, is an assistant professor in the Psychological and Quantitative Foundations Department at the University of Iowa. She received her PhD in Marriage and Family Therapy at Florida State University. Dr. Reed-Fitzke's research examines the role of risk, resilience, and relationships (e.g., family) in well-being among emerging adults, particularly among college students at risk for poor mental health and military service members. She serves as the National Council on Family Relation's Military Families and Children Focus Group cochair and has published numerous peer-reviewed articles on promoting well-being during emerging adulthood.

Julie Rodil was a bright and caring third-year student in the Health Psychology PhD program at Old Dominion University who tragically passed away February 2021. Julie had received her BS in Psychological Sciences from the College of William & Mary in 2018 and her Master's degree in Health Psychology post-humorously Spring 2021 from Old Dominion University after having defended her thesis December 2020. Julie made significant contributions to our understanding of development among adolescents and emerging adults of racial/ethnic minority groups, which includes her contribution to the current chapter, having contributed to the literature review and revision of the manuscript prior to her passing. The world has lost a bright young scholar and an amazing and caring person.

Heather T. Rowan-Kenyon, PhD, is an associate professor in the Department of Educational Leadership and Higher Education in the Lynch School of Education and Human Development at Boston College. Dr. Rowan-Kenyon's research focuses on college student access, learning, and success, particularly for first-generation college students. Her book with Ana Martínez Alemán and Mandy Savitz-Romer, *Technology and Engagement: Making Technology Work for First Generation College Students* (Rutgers University Press, 2019), was awarded the 2018 Association for the Study of Higher Education (ASHE) Outstanding Book Award.

Joan A. Swanson has a PhD in Education Psychology and Methodology from the State University of New York, University at Albany. She also has a MS in Educational Counseling and a BS in Education and Psychology. Dr. Swanson is the director of education for Franklin Pierce University and associate professor. She holds a teaching certification in nursery through 12th grade and has experience as both a school teacher and college professor teaching both education and psychology coursework. Her research interests include the study of instruction and learning, with a particular interest in emerging adults and adolescents. Dr. Swanson's research projects analyze emerging adult preferences and patterns for technology use and pedagogical practices involving technology. Additionally, Dr. Swanson authored a book chapter in which she presented her theory, "Technology as Skin," and has presented her research internationally.

Sylvia Symonds, PhD, is the associate vice president for educational outreach and student services at Arizona State University. In this role, she oversees K-12 outreach efforts and serves as the principal investigator for several grants focused on equity, college access, and student success. In all, Sylvia has over 20 years of experience supporting diverse student populations to achieve their higher education goals. An Arizona native and a first-generation college student, Sylvia received her PhD in Educational Policy and Evaluation from ASU.

Elizabeth R. Watters, MA, LMFT-t, is a doctoral candidate in the Psychological and Quantitative Foundations Department at the University of Iowa. She received her Master's in Marriage and Family Therapy at Abilene Christian University. Her research examines resilience across key developmental periods (i.e., early childhood, adolescence, emerging adulthood) for individuals with a history of childhood maltreatment. She has published peer-reviewed articles that examine childhood maltreatment, mental health, and resilience across these developmental groups.

Allison Yarri is a graduate of the Master of Arts in Higher Education Administration with a concentration in Student Affairs at Boston College, Lynch School of Education and Human Development. She received her BA in Psychology at SUNY Geneseo. She plans a career in academic advising.

Introduction

Not a Younger Version of You: How an Understanding of Emerging Adulthood Applies to Today's College Students

Tisha A. Duncan and Allison A. Buskirk-Cohen

> *Dear Professor, I am looking forward to our advising meeting this week. I wanted to let you know that my dad would be joining us if that is alright. He may have some questions too.*
>
> *—Second-Semester Freshman*

We cannot pinpoint the exact moment we began noticing changes in our students, but we have had more and more requests from students to have their parents and/or guardians present during our advising meetings. Students seem to find comfort in knowing they will not be meeting alone with the professor and that their parents can ask any questions they have as well. It certainly is a very different experience than our own and one that we have had to learn to navigate as we work with our students. In the beginning, we were defensive and at times took it personally that the students and their family members questioned our advice. However, as we began to observe our students, build relationships with them, and explore this new generation of learners, we found that their behaviors and interactions, while different than our own, were intriguing. Once we began to shift our own thinking about how education should look or feel based on our own experiences, we could see the students for who they are: individuals trying to find their own way in this world just as we did long before.

Often, adults interact with college students as if they are simply younger versions of themselves. For many people working in higher education, memories of college may evoke warm and fuzzy feelings. There may have been some challenges, but we persevered, overcame, and managed to work our way through the system to become a part of it. However, a lot of students have been failed by and are continuing to fail in the educational system. Somehow, we need to find ways to connect with those students—the ones who are not like us. While the natural trajectory of our lives leads to adulthood, the path

Tisha A. Duncan and Allison A. Buskirk-Cohen, *Introduction* In: *Cultivating Student Success*. Edited by: Tisha A. Duncan and Allison A. Buskirk-Cohen, Oxford University Press. © Oxford University Press 2022. DOI: 10.1093/oso/9780197586693.003.0001 taken and the influences of advancements in technology, social norms, and education all contribute to how people evolve and change over time. Some identities incorporate positive characteristics, such as optimism, cooperation, and other prosocial behaviors. Other identities focus on negative attributes, including narcissism and entitlement. In this introductory chapter, we aim to give the reader a better understanding of the period of adulthood, as traditionally defined, and then look more closely at the transitioning period of emerging adulthood, as defined through the work of Jeffrey Jensen Arnett. Readers will be provided with a holistic overview of the development of these young adults.

Jeffrey Jensen Arnett (2000) developed the term "emerging adulthood" to describe those in an age of transition between adolescence and adulthood, typically between the ages of 18 and 29. The defining characteristics (self-focus, instability, identity explorations, feeling in-between, and a sense of possibilities) of this age can often be viewed in a negative light. Older adults seem frustrated by what seems to be a lack of commitment by younger adults. These tensions can also arise between parents and children when they cannot decide on a major of study or career path with no long-term planning or goals. However, research has found that emerging adults are among the most socially conscious group, willing to engage in exploration, and often question traditional and archaic laws, becoming strong advocates for equity and fairness (Schwartz et al., 2013).

In the United States, we are inundated with options and decisions on a daily basis that are not limited to the basics needed for survival, but also include those choices which have long-term impacts. Emerging adults tend to have difficulty making choices and feel limited by having to choose only one path or direction (Reed et al., 2016). The majority of students in the U.S. system of higher education are in the developmental phase of emerging adulthood, yet the majority of books aimed at working with this population treat them as either children or adults. Higher education in the United States is facing a critical juncture. According to the U.S. Department of Education (2019), tuition costs are rising, while measures of success are declining. Students struggle to meet the most basic academic requirements, barely passing their courses. Other students battle physical and mental health difficulties that also impact their ability to do well in college. Many must repeat courses or fail to be retained. While institutions recognize the challenges students face, they are poorly equipped to adequately help them. Furthermore, while there is much empirical research on the factors contributing to success in higher education, there is very little information on how to apply these findings.

With the advances of technology come innovation and access to more information and people. Many members of the higher education community would identify as digital immigrants, while the students with whom they interact would identify as digital natives. In his work, Prensky (2001a, 2001b) defines "digital natives" as those from a younger generation who have been born into or brought up in the age of digital technology and are both familiar with and comfortable using it as part of their daily lives. In turn, he defines "digital immigrants" as those from an older generation who have had to learn how to use and integrate it into their lives and adapt to the age of digital technology. However, there may be false assumptions regarding the way digital natives primarily use technology, as well as discrepancies in how many students actually have access to technology (Kvavik et al., 2004).

Popular culture assumes the majority of today's college students are digital natives who have lived much of their lives with screens and platforms that document every moment. Demographic studies indicate that college students are a much more diverse group in terms of their access to and usage of technology (Kvavik et al., 2004). Therefore, the treatment of all students as digital natives, the way we currently conceptualize the term, may not be beneficial for all learners. At the same time, students enter institutions of higher education with faculty who are teaching and using traditional techniques to building relationships, instructional strategies, and approaches to learning. Examining how the availability and influence of technology have become a central component of communication and learning is critical for meaningful interactions.

This book aims to provide faculty, administrators, and staff with the knowledge and skills needed to help students succeed through integrating a developmental lens and practical application of the research, as it pertains to success to higher education. Voices and perspectives from various disciplines share research, instructional practices, and resources. The book is not intended to be an exhaustive review of research, but rather a collection of practices to work holistically with emerging adults academically, socially, and emotionally. Readers may not have a need to read the entire book sequentially but rather may identify various chapters that are related to their particular area of interest. We envision the book to be used as a resource or guide for aiding in better understanding of the age of emerging adulthood as it relates to postsecondary education. Viewing emerging adults through a positive lens allows for the discovery of their creativity, curiosity, and need for ensuring equality and fairness—qualities that benefit all. The remainder of the introduction includes summaries of each of the chapters.

Chapter 1: "I Am _____": Self-Awareness, Self-Efficacy, and Self-Motivation in Emerging Adults

Arnett contributes an intense self-focus and time of identity exploration as some of the factors to the disequilibrium felt by emerging adults. This chapter will identify how this group learns about themselves and develops confidence and the ways and means through which they find their motivation. Attention to identity development among traditionally marginalized groups and intersecting identities will be presented. For certain students, having membership in multiple identity groups means competing values, traditions, and practices. The chapter will provide an overall analysis of how identity development impacts academic success.

Chapter 2: "I Just Can't": Why are Emerging Adults Feeling More Anxious and Uncertain?

Students entering higher education self-report high levels of internalizing symptoms, such as anxiety and depression. College counseling centers confirm these mental health concerns are a significant issue that impacts academic success. This chapter will explore the social and emotional development of 18- to 29-year-olds and focus on how social emotional development contributes to feelings of anxiety, inability to make decisions, uncertainty, and lack of belonging among emerging adults. Special attention will be given to the role that identity development plays in risk and resilience during this "age of uncertainty."

Chapter 3: "We Got In!": The Influence and Role of Family on Relationships and Decision-Making

Emerging adults rely on family, friends, and others in their personal networks to aid in making decisions. Parents are heavily involved in the lives of their children, ensuring that they have all of the supports or advantages in place to become successful. Once labeled "helicopter parents" who hovered over their children at all times, some parents are now considered "lawnmower parents" who work diligently to remain one step ahead of their children to clear away any challenges, stumbling blocks, or issues. This chapter will explore how relationships between parents and their children have changed over time and what these impacts are on college and career decisions.

Chapter 4: "I Took a Screenshot": Experiences with Technology In and Out of the Classroom

There is a common assumption that screens and digital platforms have been available and used with today's college students since birth. However, research on technology use shows much more variation and complexity. This chapter will address the different experiences emerging adults have with technology both in and out of the classroom. Moreover, the impact of these experiences (or lack thereof) will be addressed.

Chapter 5: "^^ KWIM? BRB": How Do Emerging Adults Communicate Differently than Previous Generations?

What started as a way to communicate as shorthand on an online platform and via phone service has now blossomed into its own language with codes, definitions, and social norms. There has been much discussion on how this abbreviated language has and will continue to impact how people communicate orally and in formal writing situations. This chapter will examine how emerging adults communicate differently than previous generations and the impacts on their communication capabilities.

Chapter 6: "You're My Person": Building Meaningful Relationships with Emerging Adults

This chapter will identify ways to support emerging adults as they form and maintain successful social relationships. Such relationships should meet basic functional demands and help students participate socially in the campus community and be responsible for themselves and others. This chapter will look in depth at each of the critical roles of people located on the college campus who can impact and build strong relationships with emerging adults.

Chapter 7: "I've Never Had to Do This on My Own": Support to Address Retention and Success for Emerging Adults

Because emerging adults tend to struggle with feeling in-between, instability, and the need to explore who they are and from whence they have come, the transition to college can prompt anxiety and fear. Many students withdraw, are hesitant about joining new social groups, and maintain strong connections to both family and peer groups established prior to attending college. This chapter will identify ways to support emerging adults, including advising, mentoring, social programming, academic planning, etc., as they transition to the college campus.

Chapter 8: "Guiding My Success": Providing a Developmental Lens to Strengthen the Whole Person

A recurring theme for emerging adults is their desire to explore and inability to readily commit to only one idea or decision. They are constantly considering new viewpoints and perspectives, as well as their role within them as they focus on their needs and strengths. The goal of this compilation is to aid in a more in-depth level of understanding of their needs. It is also the hope that as one begins to learn more about this group of emerging adults, ages 18 to 29, there will be a shift in seeing them through a more positive lens to discover how their creativity, curiosity, and need for ensuring equality and fairness for all can be beneficial. This chapter will examine closely how the traits of emerging adults (self-focus, instability, identity explorations, feeling in-between, and a sense of possibilities) can be viewed as strengths and provide an opportunity to successfully transition into adult roles.

References

Arnett, J. J. (2000). Emerging adulthood: A theory of development from the late teens through the twenties. *American Psychologist, 55*(5), 469–480. doi:10.1037//0003-066X.55.5.469

Kvavik, R. B., Caruso, J. B., & Morgan, G. (2004). *ECAR study of students and information technology 2004: Convenience, connection, and control.* EDUCAUSE Center for Applied Research. http://www.educause.edu/ir/library/pdf/ers0405/rs/ers0405w.pdf

Prensky, M. (2001a). Digital natives, digital immigrants part 1. *On the Horizon, 9*(5), 1–6.

Prensky, M. (2001b). Digital natives, digital immigrants, part 2: Do they really think differently? *On the Horizon, 9*(6), 1–6.

Reed, K., Duncan, J. M., Lucier-Greer, M., Fixelle, C., & Ferraro, A. J. (2016). Helicopter parenting and emerging adult self-efficacy: Implications for mental and physical health. *Journal of Child and Family Studies, 25*(10), 3136–3149.

Schwartz, S. J., Zamboanga, B. L., Luyckx, K., Meca, A., & Ritchie, R. A. (2013). Identity in emerging adulthood: Reviewing the field and looking forward. *Emerging Adulthood*, *1*(2), 96–113.

U.S. Department of Education, National Center for Education Statistics. (2019). Undergraduate retention and graduation rates. In *The condition of education 2019* (NCES 2019-144). https://nces.ed.gov/programs/coe/indicator_ctr.asp

1

"I Am _____"

Self-Awareness, Self-Efficacy, and Self-Motivation in Emerging Adults

Joel A. Lane and Deanna N. Cor

The emerging adult years—generally understood as the stage of life beginning in the late teens and lasting through the 20s—represent a period of many important developmental milestones and tasks. Many of these tasks involve various forms of identity exploration, particularly in the areas of independence, career, romantic relationships, and worldview (Arnett, 2000). Identity development in these contexts occurs across a prolonged progression from adolescence to adulthood (Klimstra et al., 2012) that seems to be distinct when compared to similarly aged cohorts from previous generations (Arnett, 2000). Compared to prior cohorts, emerging adults on average significantly delay marriage and childbirth, the achievement of financial independence, and the solidification of a career identity. The psychosocial implications of these trends are such that previous theories of identity development across the lifespan (e.g., Erikson, 1968) may be less applicable to today's emerging adult populations (Lane, 2020). Accordingly, it may be useful to examine identity development in an emerging adulthood context. Such is the aim of this chapter, which will focus on identity development in emerging adulthood from the standpoints of self-awareness, self-efficacy, and self-motivation, all of which are critical outcomes of the identity development process.

Identity in Emerging Adulthood

To understand identity development in emerging adulthood, it is useful to first examine social identity theory (Tajfel & Turner, 1986). According to this theory, identity is derived through social interactions and identification with social groups. As such, it is highly applicable to the emerging adult years, a time when individuals transition their attachment systems from family to

Joel A. Lane and Deanna N. Cor, *"I Am _____"* In: *Cultivating Student Success.* Edited by: Tisha A. Duncan and Allison A. Buskirk-Cohen, Oxford University Press. © Oxford University Press 2022. DOI: 10.1093/oso/9780197586693.003.0002 peers (Fraley & Davis, 1997; Schnyders & Lane, 2018) and engage in identity exploration (Arnett, 2000). A tenet of social identity theory is that individuals are subjected to both interpersonal and intergroup influences, and that these influences can at times suggest competing social responses, creating an interpersonal-intergroup continuum along which social behaviors can vary (Tajfel & Turner, 1986). Moreover, the accumulation of responses to these interpersonal and intergroup influences gradually informs identity development. Another tenet of this theory is that all individuals strive for positive self-concept, and that this desire will further inform how the interpersonal-intergroup continuum influences identity. Higher education professionals are uniquely positioned to witness such interactions, as the college experience provides a concentrated and complex array of interpersonal and intergroup interactions (Chickering & Reisser, 1993).

In line with social identity theory, we will next examine identity development in emerging adulthood through the varying lenses of interpersonal and intergroup, which represent different and, at times, competing strands of identity literature. The interpersonal lens positions identity as a sense of self, while the intergroup lens considers identity along an intersectional framework whereby each individual is composed of a unique constellation of multicultural identities, all of which constitute forms of group influence, status, and power (Helms, 1995; Moore et al., 2020; Schwartz et al., 2011). Accordingly, it feels necessary to first consider each lens of identity separately before examining how they each inform awareness, efficacy, and motivation in emerging adulthood.

Identity as Interpersonal

A primary strand of identity development literature has centered on individualistic conceptualization. Past research in this regard has conceptualized identity formation as a clear and stable sense of self with regard to values, commitments, and goals for the future (Schwartz et al., 2011). Two important processes underlying identity formation are exploration and commitment (Marcia, 1980). Exploration refers to the active consideration of and experimentation of identity alternatives, while commitment involves the ultimate selection of and adherence to one or more of these identity alternatives (Marcia, 1980). Exploration and commitment appear to be cyclical processes whereby individuals initially explore a breadth of options and make initial commitments, and then move to exploring these commitments in greater depth before increasingly identifying with the commitments (Luyckx et al., 2006).

While identity formation was originally conceptualized as occurring in adolescence (Erikson, 1968), it seems to extend well into the emerging adult years for contemporary generations (Arnett, 2000). Today's emerging adults engage in an elongated, active process of exploring values and goals, and they take longer to form commitments compared to prior generations (Douglass, 2007). According to Arnett (2000), this prolonged process is due in part to emerging adulthood qualitatively feeling like an "in between" period of life, distinct from both adolescence and adulthood while encompassing aspects of both. That is, many emerging adults experience this period of life as combining the autonomy of adulthood with the relative freedom from adult responsibilities that is characteristic of adolescence. This dynamic offers a potential explanation for the growing sentiments among higher education personnel that contemporary cohorts of college students exhibit less maturity and overall readiness for the college experience than prior cohorts (Shatto & Erwin, 2016).

Another central aspect of emerging adulthood that interacts with identity development is the enhanced focus on self that is characteristic of this stage of life. According to emerging adulthood theory, (1) it is normative for emerging adults to exhibit enhanced self-focus, and (2) this self-focus is integral to the identity exploration process (Arnett, 2000). This enhanced self-focus is possible due to the aforementioned delaying of commitments to family and career, allowing for a moratorium of sorts from some responsibilities associated with adulthood (Layland et al., 2018). All of these factors result in emerging adults engaging in heightened focus on themselves, which aids the identity exploration process. In this regard, emerging adulthood theory contrasts substantially from other strands of research (cf. Twenge, 2013) that have conceptualized self-focus through negative conclusions about millennial and Generation Z emerging adults as being entitled and/or narcissistic (Lane, 2015a). Rather, emerging adulthood suggests that these individuals are at an earlier stage of psychosocial development than prior generations, even though expectations placed on them have remained stable over time (Arnett, 2000). For many emerging adults, navigating this discrepancy in psychosocial readiness versus societal expectations may serve as a source of psychological distress (Arnett, 2000; Lane, 2015a).

Identity as Intergroup

The preceding literature examines the developmental process of emerging adulthood through an individualistic lens whereby normative experiences occur that propel or stunt growth. However, this examination may be incomplete without also considering the impact of culture, privilege, oppression, and intersectionality on identity development. Given an emerging adult's social location and lived experiences, their pathway to understanding who they are is undoubtedly shaped by the color of their skin, their gender identity and expression, their sexuality, their socioeconomic status, their religious orientation, and many other vital and valid ways of identifying. There may exist some normative processes that cut across identity, but the ways in which an emerging adult integrates and internalizes these processes have everything to do with their personal and collective worldview.

A review of recent cross-disciplinary literature reveals that conceptualizing the experiences of emerging adults must be considered at the intersection of identities (Scroggs et al., 2018; Moore et al., 2020; Smith et al., 2019). While the salience of identity can often depend on contextual factors, identity development occurs simultaneously (e.g., race and sexuality) and and dimensions of it inherently relate to one another (Chan et al., 2018). It is vital to consider intersections of identity, but it must be made clear that the theory of intersectionality emerged from a necessity of examining how the experiences of Black women are uniquely impacted by institutional oppression such as that seen within the judicial system (Crenshaw, 1988). As such, there are further distinctive processes emerging adults with multiple minoritized identities experience as compared to emerging adults with intersections of privilege and oppression. When examining the developmental experiences of emerging adults, we must seek to avoid whitewashing and utilizing a "universal" lens as we can be sure one does not exist. Rather, taking a more critical view, while less simplified, allows for greater nuance and is likely to be more representative of the experiences of emerging adults across lived experiences. This can be difficult in institutions of higher education, many of which are making concerted efforts to attract and retain students with minoritized identities while at the same time operating with policies, procedures, and other institutional elements that often were formulated long ago and primarily by personnel with dominant cultural identities.

Examples of both commonalities and contrasts between identity development may lie within several identity development models. In the White racial identity development model, Helms (1995) posits that as part of being White in the United States, one must come into contact with folks of other races whereby personally held assumptions can be challenged, creating dissonance. The cultural identity development model, meant to embody the development of people of color in particular, examines how White supremacy requires conformity with White culture (Atkinson et al., 1979). Models that examine transgender identity development and sexual identity development both acknowledge that awareness of self is often a primary part of beginning to understand oneself (Lev, 2013). Similarly, models of identity development related to disability status acknowledge that awareness and acceptance begin the process of growth for an individual (Forber-Pratt & Zape, 2017). In contrast, Watt (2007) created a model for individuals who experience the benefits of privileged identities that involves a series of various defensive reactions that evolve as a person increases their understanding of their status in society. In essence, it is vital to recognize that emerging adults develop their understanding of who they are and want to become through exploration of self in the contexts of group affiliations and the larger society.

Self-Awareness in Emerging Adulthood

In light of these reflections on identity, the proceeding section will consider self-awareness through the lens of emerging adulthood. Self-awareness is a critical aspect of identity development, and it is useful to consider how this construct emerges and evolves during emerging adulthood. Understanding of the self is thought to be a bidirectional process between individuals and context, whereby individuals respond to life circumstances in ways that incrementally increase control over their context, gradually promoting identity commitment (Bosma & Kunnen, 2001). In this way, self-awareness can be thought of as the degree of identity commitment one has achieved. There are, however, stark contrasts in the psychosocial trajectories of emerging adults that appear to impact overall adjustment and identity commitment (Nelson & Padilla-Walker, 2013). When self-awareness is considered as bidirectional, implications for the importance of the intersections of identity emerge. An emerging adult, given context, may gain increased self-awareness about some parts of their identities more than others. For example, a White, queer emerging adult may begin to hold a nuanced understanding of gender and sexuality on a college campus, while self-awareness around racial identity may be underdeveloped.

Social relationships are a likely catalyst for these differing trajectories (Lane et al., 2017). The quality of one's social relationships is a significant factor in their ability to thrive during emerging adulthood (Lane & Fink, 2015), and it seems to be instrumental in the identity development process (Para, 2008). The ability of emerging adults to cultivate supportive social networks appears to be influenced by their attachment security (Lane & Fink, 2015). Accordingly, it is important to consider attachment in the context of emerging adulthood and its contributions to functioning and identity development during this stage of life.

Attachment security and social relationship quality appear to be fundamental to the identity development processes in emerging adulthood (e.g., Lane, 2015a; Lane et al., 2017; Schnyders & Lane, 2018). Attachment is defined as the emotional bonds that develop between children and their caregivers beginning in infancy (Bowlby, 1982). Children develop expectations regarding the degree to which their physical and emotional needs will be satisfied based on repeated experiences of caregiver responsiveness. These beliefs become internalized as subconscious representations of self and other, which continue to increase in complexity and broadly inform social interactions throughout the lifespan. As individuals reach emerging adulthood and finish high school, many aspects of the attachment system are transferred from parents and caregivers to peers and romantic partners (Fraley & Davis, 1997), though parents are often called upon for more significant forms of tangible and emotional support, particularly prior to the achievement of financial independence (Douglass, 2007). In this way, both parent and peer systems significantly impact identity development and the overall experience of emerging adulthood (Schnyders & Lane, 2018).

Longitudinal studies support the enduring nature of attachment working models during emerging adulthood, though significant life disruptions appear to have a destabilizing effect on attachment security (Waters et al., 2000). Other studies have established the relationship between attachment and social functioning in emerging adulthood. Pitman and Scharfe (2010) found that avoidant-attached emerging adults who relied primarily upon family networks experienced more distress than others relying upon family networks, and that anxious-attached individuals experienced more distress regardless of whether their primary support networks were familial or peer. Other researchers have found that attachment may be more related to perceived quality of social interactions than the actual size of one's social network (Pietromonaco & Barrett, 1997).

In addition to social functioning, attachment quality has also been demonstrated to be predictive of various measures of well-being and psychological functioning among emerging adult samples. Buhl (2007) measured the development of well-being and parental attachment in a sample of German emerging adults from their final year of college through three years of post-college life. Buhl found that, while well-being increased overall between the two assessment points, there were two distinct well-being trajectories in the sample. Parental attachment security during the participants' senior year of college was one of the main factors in predicting whether well-being increased or decreased. Other studies have established that attachment quality is predictive of psychological health and subjective well-being (Lane & Fink, 2015) and psychological distress (Mallinckrodt & Wei, 2005) during emerging adulthood.

Self-Efficacy in Emerging Adulthood

The next section will consider how emerging adults achieve self-efficacy, another outcome of identity development. Self-efficacy refers to one's belief in their ability to navigate specific circumstances and situations (Bandura, 1997). One's degree of self-efficacy can powerfully impact the ways in which individuals respond to challenges and make choices (Luszczynska & Schwarzer, 2005). Self-efficacy serves many important functions in emerging adulthood, as it is associated with well-being (Zambianchi & Bitti, 2013), career development (Guay et al., 2006), and health-oriented behaviors (Jankowska et al., 2018).

Development of self-efficacy is a primary task in emerging adulthood, a time that typically begins with increasing levels of independence and freedom from family (Sussman & Arnett, 2014). Self-efficacy appears to play an important role in other aspects of emerging adult identity development. For example, consider the aforementioned link between attachment and well-being in emerging adulthood. Self-efficacy appears to play a mediating role in this association (Jankowska et al., 2018), presumably because healthy and accepting parenting will promote positive self-concept and overall self-efficacy (Bradley-Geist & Olson-Buchanan, 2014), which in turn positively impacts one's engagement in a variety of health-oriented behaviors (Jankowska et al., 2018; Riggs et al., 2007). Self-efficacy also serves important functions in self-motivation (Schunk, 1990). People high in self-efficacy will generally experience enhanced task motivation due to believing in their capabilities to complete the task, though low self-efficacy may also motivate people to learn and gain new skills (Schunk, 1990).

There are many aspects of the emerging adult experience that moderate the development of self-efficacy in positive and negative ways. One such aspect is the common characteristic of feeling "in between" adolescence and adulthood (Arnett, 2000). The impact of this characteristic on self-efficacy development appears to be complex and multidirectional. In one sense, autonomy increases in emerging adulthood compared to adolescence due to increased independence from family (Sussman & Arnett, 2014), but on the other hand, emerging adults are often faced with increasing adult responsibilities for which they may or may not be developmentally ready (Lane, 2015a), which can threaten self-efficacy (Lane, 2015b). Experiences with racism and discrimination also influence a person's self-efficacy. A study examining the identity development processes of Muslim Americans found that to defend against anti-Muslim vitriol, they needed to take a "defensive" stance and present as cohesive and homogenous (Wang et al., 2020, p. 344). Identity development often involves the ability to test behaviors and beliefs, allowing an emerging adult to become adept at maintaining a sense of self and group membership. Experiences with racism and discrimination require a person to navigate complex dynamics that likely promote self-efficacy and may deny some aspects of exploration.

Another feature of emerging adulthood that can impact self-efficacy is the high degree of significant life transitions that occur during this stage of life. Between the ages of 18 and 29, it is common for emerging adults to graduate high school, leave home (often moving back in and leaving again several times; cf. Goldscheider & Goldscheider, 1999), and enter a professional environment. Moreover, many emerging adults enter and leave college during this time. With each of these transitions comes significant life change, as they involve changes in social networks, familial support, and autonomy. For some emerging adults, many of these experiences can also prompt psychological distress (Lane et al., 2017; Mallinckrodt & Wei, 2005), which is of particular concern given the aforementioned connection between emerging adulthood and problematic responses to stress. The experience of life transitions reduces perceived environmental mastery—a construct with many parallels to self-efficacy—and other aspects of psychological well-being in emerging adulthood (Lane et al., 2017). Attachment and social relationship quality are important to the relative success emerging adults experience as they navigate life transitions (Lane & Fink, 2015).

Closely connected to self-efficacy, the imposter phenomenon (Clance & Imes, 1978) is an experience that one is incompetent despite evidence of competence. Individuals experiencing imposter phenomenon attribute evidence of competence to luck, are unable to internalize sources of competence, and maladaptively require validation and praise from others (Lane, 2015b). Moreover, the imposter phenomenon promotes feelings of fraudulence, causing individuals to perceive that their abilities are overestimated and that others will eventually discover their incompetence (Clance & Imes, 1978). While the imposter experience may seem synonymous with low self-efficacy, there are conceptual and empirical distinctions. Conceptually, while someone low in self-efficacy would likely doubt their abilities, someone with imposter experiences would likely doubt their abilities despite evidence supporting their competence. Empirically, prior research suggests that gaining professional experience increases self-efficacy but does not impact imposter feelings (Royse-Rokowski, 2010). There exists preliminary evidence that the imposter phenomenon is substantially more prevalent in emerging adulthood compared to other age groups, and it may be especially pronounced during the transition to career (Lane, 2015b).

Self-Motivation in Emerging Adulthood

As a final consideration of identity development in emerging adulthood, we will consider self-motivation. Motivation is an important precursor to participation and achievement, as it informs the purpose, enthusiasm, and enduringness of activity (Skinner et al., 2009). We are thought to have motivation when tasks seem useful, important, interesting, and worthy of our energy (Eccles et al., 2015). Conversely, amotivation can occur when we feel tasks lack value and interest and when we feel unable to master them (Shen et al., 2010), and it is a powerful predictor of inaction (Cheon & Reeve, 2015). Age-related transitions, in which one transfers to a different sociocultural context at a similar age, seem to be critical periods for motivation development (Symonds et al., 2019).

The concept of emerging adulthood as a critical period for motivation development suggests the presence of distinct motivational trajectories across this period of life. In support of this idea, Nelson and Padilla-Walker (2013) used a large emerging adult sample to identify three distinct adjustment trajectories, including well adjusted, poorly adjusted, and externalizing. It appears that well-adjusted emerging adults are able to explore and internalize belief systems and engage in fewer risk behaviors, while poorly adjusted emerging adults experience higher levels of depression and anxiety, and externalizing emerging adults engage in higher levels of substance use. Importantly, those in the well-adjusted class demonstrated higher levels of identity commitment than did those in the externalizing and poorly adjusted classes. It appeared that participants in the study were having different emerging adulthood experiences partially as a function of motivation. That is, the well-adjusted group was theorized to have more prosocial attitudes, while the other groups were thought to be responding to different motivational stimuli: namely, internal and external stressors. We would be remiss not to acknowledge the impact power, privilege, and oppression have on motivation. Those working closely with emerging adults must always be curious about the impact of discrimination and bias on motivation, identity development, and well-being.

The most common contexts where motivation applies in emerging adulthood are relational, career, and academic, all of which are subjected to substantial transition in emerging adulthood (Lane & Fink, 2015). Given that these transitions are critical periods for well-being and opportunities to utilize coping skills, it follows that self-motivation is key to developing beliefs and attitudes that could help emerging adults persevere during transition (Skinner et al., 2009). However, not all motivation contexts in emerging adulthood are transition related. Emerging adults have increasingly turned their attention and efforts to political and social activism (Seemiller & Grace, 2015). This is especially true for Generation Z, who demonstrate unprecedented levels of desire for and action toward progressive social change (Seemiller & Grace, 2015; Tanaid & Wright, 2019). According to Arnett (2000), a defining characteristic of the emerging adulthood experience is a sense of optimism about future possibilities. It may be that today's emerging adults are more motivated by possibilities in the collective sense, motivating them to pursue social justice (Arnett, 2013). Activism and community engagement have long been theorized to be instrumental to the identity development process (Erikson, 1968). Research suggests that identity is instrumental to emerging adult motivation for community involvement, which reciprocally influences identity development (Hardy et al., 2011). Community involvement also contributes to moral and civic identity development (Pratt et al., 2003).

Conclusion

The emerging adult years represent a distinct period of life during which many critical identity development processes occur. These processes interact with the various dimensions of the emerging adult experience, including demographic instability, subjectively feeling "in between" adolescence and adulthood, prolonged identity exploration, increased self-focus, and subjectively experiencing emerging adulthood as a time of possibilities. Identity is also influenced by group affiliation, with important implications for privilege and oppression. Self-awareness, self-efficacy, and self-motivation are all important outcomes of emerging adult identity development, which can be impacted by attachment and social relationship quality, as well as the experience of life transitions in emerging adulthood. Higher education personnel must consider these dynamics when engaging with students, crafting and enforcing policies and procedures, and critically examining existing practices.

Guiding Questions

1. Consider your own intersecting identities (i.e., race, gender, sexuality, ability status, religion, economic/educational, etc.). How has your sense of self been shaped by those identities?
2. Think about your earliest memories of your cultural identities. Who in your life helped to define your identities?
3. The significance of identity is context dependent. Given your most frequent context (i.e., school, work, home), which parts of your identity are most significant? How might that significance impact your view of self?

Questions for emerging adults:

1. What do you have "figured out" about life that you did not know when you were a teenager? What do you still need to "figure out"?
2. In what situations are you most motivated? Least motivated?

References

Arnett, J. J. (2000). Emerging adulthood: A theory of development from the late teens through the twenties. *American Psychologist, 55*(5), 469–480. doi:10.1037//0003-066X.55.5.469

Arnett, J. J. (2013). The evidence for Generation We and against Generation Me. *Emerging Adulthood, 1*(1), 5–10. doi:10.1177/2167696812466842

Atkinson, D. R., Morten, G., & Sue, D. W. (Eds.). (1979). *Counseling American minorities*. McGraw-Hill.

Bandura, A. (1997). *Self-efficacy: The exercise of control*. Freeman.

Bosma, H. A., & Kunnen, S. E. (2001). Determinants and mechanisms in ego identity development: A review and synthesis. *Developmental Review, 21*, 39–66.

Bowlby, J. (1982). *Attachment and loss* (Vol. I). Basic Books.

Bradley-Geist, J. C., & Olson-Buchanan, J. B. (2014). Helicopter parents: An examination of the correlates of over-parenting of college students. *Education and Training, 56*, 314–328. doi:10.1108/ET10-2012-0096

Buhl, H. M. (2007). Well-being and the child-parent relationship at the transition from university to work life. *Journal of Adolescent Research, 22*(5), 550–571. doi:10.1177/0743558407305415

Chan, C. D., Cor, D. N., & Band, M. P. (2018). Privilege and oppression in counselor education: An intersectionality framework. *Journal of Multicultural Counseling and Development, 46*(1), 58–73.

Cheon, S. H., & Reeve, J. (2015). A classroom-based intervention to help teachers decrease students' amotivation. *Contemporary Educational Psychology, 40*, 99–111. https://doi.org/10.1016/j.cedpsych.2014.06.004

Chickering, A. W., & Reisser, L. (1993). *Education and identity* (2nd ed.). Jossey-Bass.

Clance, P. R., & Imes, S. A. (1978). The imposter phenomenon among high achieving women: Dynamics and therapeutic intervention. *Psychotherapy Theory, Research, and Practice, 15*, 241–247.

Crenshaw, K. (1988). Race, reform, and retrenchment: Transformation and legitimation in antidiscrimination law. *Harvard Law Review, 101*, 1331–1387.

Douglass, C. B. (2007). From duty to desire: Emerging adulthood in Europe and its consequences. *Child Development Perspectives, 1*(2), 101–108.

Eccles, J. S., Fredricks, J., & Baay, P. (2015). Expectancies, values, identities, and self-regulation. In G. Oettingen & P. M. Gollwitzer (Eds.), *Self-regulation in adolescence* (pp. 30–56). Cambridge University Press.

Erikson, E. (1968). *Identity: Youth and crisis*. Norton.

Forber-Pratt, A. J., & Zape, M. P. (2017). Disability identity development model: Voices from the ADA-generation. *Disability and Health Journal, 10*(2), 350–355. doi:10.1016/j.dhjo.2016.12.013

Fraley, R. C., & Davis, K. E. (1997). Attachment formation and transfer in young adults' close friendships and romantic relationships. *Personal Relationships, 4*(2), 131–144. doi:10.1111/j.1475-6811.1997.tb00135.x

Goldscheider, F., & Goldscheider, C. (1999). *Leaving home: The changing transition to adulthood*. Sage.

Guay, F., Ratelle, C. F., Senécal, C., Larose, S., & Deschênes, A. (2006). Distinguishing developmental from chronic career indecision: Self-efficacy, autonomy, and social support. *Journal of Career Assessment, 14*(2), 235–251. doi:org/10.1177/1069072705283975

Hardy, S. A., Pratt, M. W., Pancer, S. M., Olsen, J. A., & Lawford, H. L. (2011). Community and religious involvement as contexts of identity change across late adolescence and emerging adulthood. *International Journal of Behavioral Development, 35*(2), 125–135.

Helms, J. E. (1995). An update of Helm's White and people of color racial identity models. In J. G. Ponterotto, J. M. Casas, L. A. Suzuki, & C. M. Alexander (Eds.), *Handbook of multicultural counseling* (pp. 181–198). Sage Publications.

Jankowska, A., M., Łockiewicz, M., Dykalska-Bieck, D., Łada, A., Owoc, W., & Stańczykowski, D. (2018). Health behaviours in emerging adulthood: Their relationship with perceived maternal and paternal parental attitudes and the mediating role of self-efficacy. *Health Psychology Report, 6*(1), 94–108. https://doi.org/10.5114/hpr.2018.71202

Klimstra, T. A., Luyckx, K., Germeijs, V., Meeus, W. H. J., & Goossens, L. (2012). Personality traits and educational identity formation in late adolescents: Longitudinal associations and academic progress. *Journal of Youth and Adolescence, 41*, 346–361.

Lane, J. A. (2015a). Counseling emerging adults in transition: Practical applications of attachment and social support research. *Professional Counselor, 5*(1), 15–27. doi:10.15241/jal.5.1.15

Lane, J. A. (2015b). The imposter phenomenon among emerging adults transitioning into professional life: Developing a grounded theory. *Adultspan Journal, 14*(2), 114–128. doi:10.1002/adsp.12009

Lane, J. A. (2020). Attachment, ego resilience, emerging adulthood, social resources, and well-being among traditional-aged college students. *Professional Counselor, 10*(2), 157–169. doi:10.15241/jal.10.2.157

Lane, J. A., & Fink, R. S. (2015). Attachment, social support satisfaction, and well-being during life transition in emerging adulthood. *Counseling Psychologist, 43*(7), 1034–1058. doi:10.1177/0011000015592184

Lane, J. A., Leibert, T. W., & Goka-Dubose, E. (2017). The impact of life transition on emerging adult attachment, social support, and well-being: A multiple group analysis. *Journal of Counseling and Development, 95*(4), 378–388. doi:10.1002/jcad.12153

Layland, E. K., Hill, B. J., & Nelson, L. J. (2018). Freedom to explore the self: How emerging adults use leisure to develop identity. *Journal of Positive Psychology, 13*(1), 78–91. doi:10.1080/17439760.2017.1374440

Lev, A. I. (2013). *Transgender emergence: Therapeutic guidelines for working with gender-variant people and their families.* Routledge.

Luszczynska, A., & Schwarzer, R. (2005). Social cognitive theory. In M. Conner & P. Norman (Eds.), *Predicting health behavior* (2nd ed.). Open University Press.

Luyckx, K., Goossens, L., & Soenens, B. (2006). A developmental-contextual perspective on identity construction in emerging adulthood: Change dynamics in commitment formation and commitment evaluation. *Developmental Psychology, 42,* 366–380. http://dx.doi.org/10.1037/0012-1649.42.2.366

Mallinckrodt, B., & Wei, M. (2005). Attachment, social competencies, social support, and psychological distress. *Journal of Counseling Psychology, 52*(3), 358–367. doi:10.1037/0022-0167.52.3.358

Marcia, J. E. (1980). Identity in adolescence. In J. Adelson (Ed.), *Handbook of adolescent psychology.* Wiley.

Moore, K. L., Camacho, D., & Munson, M. R. (2020). Identity negotiation processes among Black and Latinx sexual minority young adult mental health service users. *Journal of Gay & Lesbian Social Services, 32*(1), 21–48.

Nelson, L. J., & Padilla-Walker, L. M. (2013). Flourishing and floundering in emerging adult college students. *Emerging Adulthood, 1*(1), 67–78. doi:10.1177/2167696812470938

Para, E. A. (2008). The role of social support in identity formation: A literature review. *Graduate Journal of Counseling Psychology, 1*(1), 97–105.

Pietromonaco, P. R., & Barrett, L. F. (1997). Working models of attachment and daily social interactions. *Journal of Personality and Social Psychology, 73*(6), 1409–1423. doi:10.1037/0022-3514.73.6.1409

Pitman, R., & Scharfe, E. (2010). Testing the function of attachment hierarchies during emerging adulthood. *Personal Relationships, 17*(2), 201–216. doi:10.1111/j.1475- 6811.2010.01272.x

Pratt, M. W., Hunsberger, B., Pancer, S. M., & Alisat, S. (2003). A longitudinal analysis of personal values socialization: Correlates of a moral self-ideal in late adolescence. *Social Development, 12*(4), 563–585. doi:10.1111/sode.2003.12.issue-4

Riggs, N., Sakuma, K., & Pentz, M. (2007). Preventing risk for obesity by promoting self-regulation and decision-making skills: Pilot results from the PATH-WAYS to health program (PATHWAYS). *Evaluation Review, 31,* 287–310. doi:10.1177/0193841X06297243

Royse-Roskowski, J. C. (2010). *Imposter phenomenon and counseling self-efficacy: The impact of imposter feelings* [Unpublished doctoral dissertation]. Ball State University. http://cardinalscholar.bsu.edu/handle/123456789/194625

Schnyders, C., & Lane, J. A. (2018). Gender, parent and peer relationships, and identification with emerging adulthood among college students. *Journal of College Counseling, 21*(3), 239–251. doi:10.1002/jocc.12106

Schunk, D. H. (1990). Goal setting and self-efficacy during self-regulated learning. *Educational Psychologist, 25,* 71–86. doi:10.1207/s15326985ep2501_6

Schwartz, S. J., Luyckx, K., & Vignoles, V. L. (Eds.). (2011). *Handbook of identity theory and research.* Springer.

Scroggs, B., Miller, J. M., & Hunter Stanfield, M. (2018). Identity development and integration of religious identities in gender and sexual minority emerging adults. *Journal for the Scientific Study of Religion, 57*(3), 604–615.

Seemiller, C., & Grace, M. (2015). *Generation Z goes to college.* Jossey-Bass.

Shatto, B., & Erwin, K. (2016). Moving on from Millennials: Preparing for Generation Z. *Journal of Continuing Education in Nursing, 47*(6), 253–254.

Shen, B., Li, W., Sun, H., & Rukavina, P. (2010). The influence of inadequate teacher-to-student social support on amotivation of physical education students. *Journal of Teaching in Physical Education, 29*(4), 417–432. doi:10.1123/jtpe.29.4.417

Skinner, E. A., Kindermann, T. A., Connell, J. P., & Wellborn, J. G. (2009). Engagement as an organizational construct in the dynamics of motivational development. In K. Wentzel & A. Wigfield (Eds.), *Handbook of motivation in school* (pp. 223–245). Routledge.

Smith, K. C., Boakye, B., Williams, D., & Fleming, L. (2019). The exploration of how identity intersectionality strengthens STEM identity for Black female undergraduates attending a historically black college and university (HBCU). *Journal of Negro Education, 88*(3), 407–418.

Sussman, S., & Arnett, J. J. (2014). Emerging adulthood: Developmental period facilitative of the addictions. *Evaluation & the Health Professions, 37,* 147–155. doi:10.1177/0163278714521812

Symonds, J. E., Schoon, I., Eccles, J. S., & Salmela-Aro, K. (2019). The development of motivation and amotivation to study and work across age-related transitions in adolescence and young adulthood. *Journal of Youth and Adolescence, 48,* 1131–1145. https://doi.org/10.1007/s10964-019-01003-4

Tajfel, H., & Turner, J. C. (1986). The social identity theory of intergroup behavior. In S. Worchel & W. G. Austin (Eds.), *Psychology of intergroup relations* (pp. 7–24). Nelson-Hall.

Tanaid, K. L., & Wright, K. L. (2019). The intersection between Chickering's theory and Generation Z student of color activism. *Vermont Connection, 40,* 15. https://scholarworks.uvm.edu/tvc/vol40/iss1/15

Twenge, J. M. (2013). The evidence for Generation Me and against Generation We. *Emerging Adulthood, 1*(1), 11–16. doi:10.1177/2167696812466548

Wang, S. C., Raja, A. H., & Azhar, S. (2020). "A lot of us have a very difficult time reconciling what being Muslim is": A phenomenological study on the meaning of being Muslim American. *Cultural Diversity and Ethnic Minority Psychology, 26*(3), 338–346. http://dx.doi.org/10.1037/cdp0000297

Waters, E., Merrick, S., Treboux, D., Crowell, J., & Albersheim, L. (2000). Attachment security from infancy to early adulthood: A twenty-year longitudinal study. *Child Development, 71*(3), 684–689. doi:10.1111/1467-8624.00176

Watt, S. K. (2007). Difficult dialogues, privilege and social justice: Uses of the Privileged Identity Exploration (PIE) Model in student affairs practice. *College and Student Affairs Journal, 26*(2), 114–126.

Zambianchi, M., & Bitti, P. E. R. (2013). The role of proactive coping strategies, time perspective, perceived efficacy on affect regulation, divergent thinking and family communication in promoting social well-being in emerging adulthood. *Social Indicators Research, 116*(2), 493–507. doi:10.1007/sl 1205-013-0307-x

2

"I Just Can't"

Why are Emerging Adults Feeling More Anxious and Uncertain?

Alan Meca, Kelsie Allison, Julie Rodil, Kenneth L. Ayers, and Kyle Eichas

As the transition to adulthood has become more individually directed and less socially prescribed (Schwartz, Côté, & Arnett, 2005), the challenge of navigating this unstructured period can be overwhelming without the proper support (Schwartz, 2016), leading some youth to believe, "I just can't." It is not surprising that anxiety and depression represent the most common mental health concerns among college students (Collegiate Mental Health [CCMH], 2019). Indeed, a large portion of college students reported feeling tremendous stress (56%), hopeless (52%), overwhelming anxiety (61%), lonely (63%), sad (67%), and mentally exhausted (88%) within the last 12 months (American College Health Association [ACHA], 2018). Additionally, 42% of college students reported feeling so depressed that it was difficult to function, and 12% seriously considered suicide within the last 12 months (ACHA, 2018). Even more troubling, studies indicate that anxiety and depression are becoming more prevalent among college students (Kitzrow, 2003). As a result, emerging adulthood has been increasingly conceptualized as a time of divergent psychosocial pathways, with identity playing a critical role in which way a person will go (Schwartz, 2016). The current chapter outlines the impact identity has on mental health, provides a case study of an identity-focused intervention by which we may support youths' identity development, and concludes with recommendations for professionals working with college students.

Identity and Psychosocial Functioning in an Age of Uncertainty

As a whole, identity has been increasingly conceptualized as a "steering mechanism" that guides one's life pathways and decisions (Eichas et al., 2014) and

Alan Meca, Kelsie Allison, Julie Rodil, Kenneth L. Ayers, and Kyle Eichas, *"I Just Can't"* In: *Cultivating Student Success.*
Edited by: Tisha A. Duncan and Allison A. Buskirk-Cohen, Oxford University Press. © Oxford University Press 2022.
DOI: 10.1093/oso/9780197586693.003.0003

serves as an anchor during periods of uncertainty and life transitions (Meca et al., 2017; Meca, Rodil, et al., 2019). During emerging adulthood, youths are no longer constrained by childhood structures and have the freedom to explore new possibilities in developing their identity (Arnett, 2000). Many emerging adults encounter numerous opportunities and possibilities that provide increased potential for positive development through purposeful *exploration* (i.e., sorting through various potential identity alternatives) that is followed by enacting a set of life *commitments* (i.e., selecting and adhering to one or more such alternatives) that helps to reduce worry and anxiety in a period of uncertainty (Luyckx et al., 2008). However, re-evaluating past choices and exploring new life directions can also increase the risk for identity-related uncertainty or distress (Crocetti et al., 2009) and has adverse effects on psychosocial and health outcomes (Schwartz et al., 2015). To follow, we review the literature linking identity development to distress/internalizing symptoms (i.e., symptoms of depression and anxiety) and well-being. Moreover, because the developmental and cultural contexts for identity work during emerging adulthood differ across countries (Schwartz et al., 2015), we focus on research with U.S. college student populations.

Marcia's (1966) identity status model has provided a durable framework for understanding identity development among college students. (Additional information on identity development can be found in Chapter 1 of this book.) Working within this framework, Waterman et al. (2013) utilized tertiary splits to categorize college students into achieved (i.e., a set of commitments enacted following exploration), foreclosure (i.e., a set of commitments enacted without prior exploration), moratorium (i.e., a state of active exploration with few commitments), and diffused (i.e., an absence of commitments coupled with a lack of interest in exploration) categories. Although foreclosures and achievers were equivalent across a variety of well-being outcomes, internalizing symptoms were lowest among those in the foreclosure status, followed by those in the achieved status. However, those in the achieved status had significantly higher levels of internal locus of control. In contrast to this theory-driven approach, Schwartz et al. (2011) utilized a data-driven approach to identify six unique clusters of identity status: achievement, searching moratorium, foreclosure, diffused diffusion, carefree diffusion, and undifferentiated. Although symptoms of depression and general anxiety were lower among foreclosure than those in the achievement status, a variety of indicators of well-being were significantly higher among those in the achievement over the foreclosure status.

These findings emphasize that enacting a set of life commitments helps to reduce worry and anxiety during this period of uncertainty, regardless of whether youth have experienced a period of exploration or not. However, the fact that identity achievement was associated with higher levels of well-being, in terms of psychological and eudaimonic well-being (Schwartz et al., 2011) and locus of control (Schwartz et al., 2011; Waterman et al., 2013), may indicate that foreclosure is adaptive as long as the person is able to rely on established norms and standards (Schwartz et al., 2015). In contrast to foreclosures, achievers may have an increased ability or tendency to adapt to changing life circumstances. Indeed, prior studies have indicated that individuals with an identity achieved status are more likely to utilize an active critical problem-solving approach to constructing a sense of self (Berzonsky & Neimeyer, 1994). However, it is important to note that Ritchie et al. (2013) found that commitment, after controlling for well-being, was positively associated with internalizing symptoms. These findings emphasize that identity commitments are not inherently good or bad. Instead, the association of commitment with psychosocial functioning may depend on what commitment is being made. Indeed, committing to a personally meaningful set of goals, values, and beliefs may be linked with well-being, whereas commitment to maladaptive identities, such as a negative identity (Hihara et al., 2018), is likely to produce negative psychosocial functioning.

At the same time, both Waterman et al. (2013) and Schwartz et al. (2011) found that the diffused statuses were associated with the lowest levels of well-being and highest levels of internalizing symptoms. However, it is important to note that in contrast to Waterman et al. (2013), the data-driven approach utilized by Schwartz et al. (2011) identified two types of diffusion, a carefree diffusion and a diffused diffusion. The extraction of two types of diffusion is consistent with Erikson's (1968) distinction between those who struggle to establish a coherent identity (i.e., diffused diffusion) and those who are simply uninterested in identity development. Such findings are consistent with prior research among Italian (Crocetti et al., 2011) and Dutch (Luyckx et al., 2008) college students. However, whereas prior studies have indicated that those in the carefree diffused status have comparable outcomes to those in the achieved and foreclosure status among Dutch college students (Luyckx et al., 2008), Schwartz et al. (2011) found well-being lowest among those in the carefree diffused status and that they had comparable levels of internalizing symptoms to the diffused diffusion status. Such findings highlight that, regardless of whether one's lack of commitment stems from difficulty establishing a sense of self (i.e., diffused diffusion) or a disinterest (i.e., carefree diffused), within the highly individualist context of the United States (Hofstede, 2015), a coherent sense of self is necessary for navigating this unstructured period of the lifespan. Finally, across both Waterman et al. (2013)

and Schwartz et al. (2011), those individuals in the moratorium status were typically associated with levels of internalizing symptoms and well-being that were either comparable to those in the diffused status or slightly improved.

Conclusion

As a whole, these findings indicate that the process of exploring one's sense of self likely involves entering into a state of confusion that may temporarily destabilize individuals as they seek to make lasting commitments (Schwartz et al., 2015). However, it is worth noting that identity development often involves navigating a period of identity uncertainty (Erikson, 1968). Indeed, Schwartz et al. (2009) found that while present exploration was strongly associated with increased identity confusion, past exploration was negatively associated with identity confusion, which in turn was negatively associated with well-being and positively associated with internalizing symptoms. At the same time, recent evidence has indicated that internalizing symptoms may compromise identity development (Meca, Rodil, al., 2019). Put another way, prolonged exploration coupled with severe identity distress may lead to a diffused sense of self marked by long-term anxiety and depressive symptoms (Kroger & Marcia, 2011).

A Case Study: The Miami Adult Development Project

As previously noted, for those who establish a sense of self and identity, this age represents a period of possibility and positive psychosocial functioning (Schwartz et al., 2015). However, navigating this period may be overwhelming, leading some to believe, "I just can't." Côté (2019) argues that such beliefs are rooted in a disempowering cultural narrative about mental health that, drawing from the medical model of psychotherapy, pathologizes challenging experiences. An alternative approach is to adopt an existential-psychosocial narrative about purpose and identity to guide work with young people (Côté, 2019). Toward this end, numerous youth development programs have targeted positive identity development (Eichas et al., 2017). We define *positive identity development* as the proactive, relational process of making choices about goals, roles, beliefs, and values and enacting these choices in ways that create narrative coherence and an overarching sense of direction and purpose (Eichas et al., 2014). Among such interventions (for a review, see Eichas et al., 2014), we turn our attention to the Miami Adult

Development Project (Miami-ADP), which was specifically developed for work with emerging adults (Meca et al., 2014), as an exemplar case study for how we may promote positive development.

The Miami-ADP was a classroom-based, peer-led program that sought to help participants to clarify and optimize their unique potentials and work through identity-related uncertainty by supporting two forms of identity exploration: self-construction and self-discovery. *Self-construction* refers to the process by which individuals create the self through identity-related choices made from alternatives afforded by their context (Eichas et al., 2014). As a result, self-construction requires cognitive and communicative competencies, including critical thinking and discussion, to interpret and organize self-relevant information (Berzonsky, 2016). In contrast, *self-discovery* refers to the process by which individuals discover and actualize their unique potentials, talents, skills, and capabilities (Eichas et al., 2014). Whereas self-construction has been conceptualized as a cognitive process, self-discovery has been conceptualized as an emotion-focused process involving one's feeling or intuition that an activity resonates with their true self (Berzonsky, 2016).

The Miami-ADP (Meca et al., 2014) combined self-discovery and self-construction with the group processes of engagement and participatory colearning. Engagement refers to building connectedness and cohesion among group members, whereas participatory colearning refers to working together to identify important life challenges and potential solutions. The goal of combining these group processes with identity processes was to facilitate transformative actions. These actions aim at overcoming life challenges and pursuing life goals, thereby enhancing a sense of mastery over life challenges and goals and reducing the stress associated with the uncertainty and lack of structure associated with emerging adulthood. A Life Course Journal (see Table 2.1) consisting of a set of exercises was used to help participants integrate the group processes, identity processes, and transformative actions they experienced into a coherent narrative about "who I am" and "what I want to do with my life" (Eichas et al., 2014).

The first exercise focused on participants' life course narratives. Participants shared with each other where they came from, where they are currently, and where they are going in their lives, as well as important life events and turning points. This exercise helped participants experience giving and receiving support, while also highlighting their commonalities. The second exercise focused on participants' most important life goals. Participants helped each other explore their life goals, identify activities essential for achieving the goals, and become aware of the feelings that arose when an activity resonated with the true self, leading to self-discovery. The third exercise focused

Table 2.1. Description of Life Course Journal Exercises

Phase	Exercise	Description
Engagement	Exercise 1	Participants identify their most important life course events and turning points and co-construct their life stories, taking turns sharing with the group
	Exercise 2	Participants build on the emerging narrative frame by identifying their most important life goal, breaking these goals into activities essential for achieving the goal, and exploring their emotional reactions to engaging in the activities
Participatory colearning	Exercise 3	Group members conceptualize their life change goals, share them with the group so they can see how their life change goals overlap (or do not overlap), and envision how the group would be different if members accomplished their life change goals
	Exercise 4	Group members create a path toward their life change goals by co-constructing with the group potential alternatives for accomplishing the life change goal and critically evaluating these alternatives. Selected solutions that emerge from this process represent potential transformative activities

on participants' life *change* goals. Participants helped each other conceptualize the changes they wanted to make in their present lives and envision how the group would be different if members accomplished these life change goals. Finally, the fourth exercise focused on critical problem solving. Participants worked together to co-construct strategies for accomplishing their life change goals by discussing and evaluating multiple possible strategies (i.e., self-construction). In this exercise, participants used a tool called ICED (Identify the Problem, Create Alternatives, Evaluate Alternatives, and Do Something) to facilitate critical thinking and discussion.

Currently, we are implementing an adaptation of the Miami-ADP as a service-learning program in Waco, Texas, for working-class college students that adds two action components: the hands-on experience of mentoring adolescents (targeting self-discovery) and the collaborative exploration of career and education possibilities (targeting self-construction). The Waco-ADP starts with peer-facilitated groups guided by the Life Course Journal. Then, after a period of training, participants become mentors and facilitate small mentoring groups composed of low-income adolescents who would be first in their families to go to college. At the same time, the participants explore their futures by researching potential graduate school programs, engaging in collaborative conversations about them, and preparing application materials.

Several additional exercises help students consolidate their experiences and integrate them into their developing life course narrative. At the end of each semester of mentoring, students write narrative descriptions of their best and worst mentoring sessions of the semester, as well as the subjective meaning and significance of these experiences. At the end of the year, mentors pair up and conduct an adapted version of the Life Course Interview (Arango et al., 2008) with each other as a way of integrating their mentoring experiences into their larger life course narrative. Finally, students write a "Letter to the Next Mentor" in which they provide guidance to the next cohort of mentors, leaving a legacy of their year's work.

The narratives that emerge out of the end-of-year Life Course Interview provide insight into how positive identity interventions can change lives for the better. For example, one mentor, a 23-year-old Hispanic female who was first in her family to get a bachelor's degree and who has subsequently entered graduate school, described how she is reauthoring her life story:

> I have become pretty proud of myself and have surprised myself with the interview for the counseling [graduate] program and I have become proud because I have proven to myself that I do have strengths and not just weaknesses. It's crazy to see I am going to start my next chapter. And just last semester I thought around this time I would be waiting to be a makeup artist or that I wouldn't get accepted into a [graduate] program.

She described how she used being a mentor to expand and enhance an aspect of her life story that was meaningful to her and refine her sense of direction and purpose:

> I decided to major in psychology and become a counselor because I wanted to hear people when they weren't being heard. . . . Being a mentor confirmed and pushed me to continue on with my education, showing how many people need and want someone to be there for them that care for their well-being. Mentoring had a great involvement in deciding my future.

When asked about what going to college meant to her, she emphasized the vital role that her relationships with peers and professors played in helping her chart her life course:

College helped me grow, helped me decide to stick with the career I started with, instead of going to be a makeup artist like I thought would happen after finishing with my bachelor's degree. Instead, college—the peers and professors—have helped me and pushed me to go to graduate school, with some purposefully pushing and some not realizing their impact.

Recommendations for Professionals

After reviewing identity theory and identity interventions, we now draw on this literature to provide professionals with recommendations for promoting positive development for college-attending emerging adults.

Identity Development Requires Time

The establishment of a coherent sense of self is a developmental process that unfolds over time. Although the first steps toward forming a sense of identity occur in adolescence, the most intensive identity exploration occurs during emerging adulthood (Arnett, 2007). As a result, it is important to understand that undergraduate freshmen and sophomores are in the early phases of exploring their sense of self before making identity commitments. Therefore, it is imperative that we provide a supportive context for students to have the opportunity for an extended moratorium, as rushing commitments could result in identity foreclosure (Schwartz, 2016).

Build Identity-Supportive Relationships

As discussed, Erikson (1968) posited that a sense of self and identity emerges through interactions between the individual and their social context. Relationships between students and university personnel play a role in shaping identity development. Healthy identity development emerges from a balance between individuality and a sense of belongingness (Koepke & Denissen, 2012), which is maintained through frequent positive contact with others and reliable parent-child relationships (Baumeister & Leary, 1995). Additionally, the process of proactive identity exploration often involves gathering information from advisors and mentors. As professionals working with college-attending emerging adults, it is important that we recognize the impact our interactions have on identity development. Indeed, research on science identity, a predictor of success and retention (Carlone & Johnson, 2007), found that the establishment of a science identity is contingent on being recognized by others as capable and competent within their discipline. Thus, it is important we affirm and recognize students' potentials and capacities. Additionally, for students struggling to solidify an identity commitment, it is important that we encourage proactive exploration into new domains and challenge students to reconsider aspects of their identity.

Create Opportunities for Self-Construction and Self-Discovery

It is important to encourage proactive identity exploration by integrating opportunities for self-construction and self-discovery into academic advising and introductory courses. Beyond the intervention activities discussed earlier (see Eichas et al., 2014), one strategy for supporting self-discovery is to raise students' awareness of identity-relevant emotional information from experiences that have produced high levels of enjoyment in the past. For example, former high school athletes may no longer entertain dreams of becoming professional athletes, but they can probably identify personally expressive features of their athletic experiences—perhaps taking on difficult personal challenges or contributing to the collective effort of a team—that they might want to expand in their present life and incorporate into a future career. Another strategy is to introduce students to new experiences that have the potential to generate feelings of personal expressiveness, such as connecting students to internships and service-learning opportunities and building applied learning experiences into classes. As students gain increased awareness of what activities fit their unique strengths and potentials, they can use this knowledge to enhance self-constructive exploration of possible future life directions. For example, rather than pursing educational and career pathways because they fit the expectations of parents or peers, they can evaluate possible education and career alternatives for their potential to produce feelings of personal expressiveness and, ultimately, enhance happiness.

Sociocultural Context Matters

As a final note, it is important to recognize that identity is constrained by its cultural and historical context (Erikson, 1968). Building on this basic premise, in the following section we focus on two important avenues necessary for contextualizing our understanding of identity development. First, we emphasize that existing identity literature is limited largely to Western, European, industrialized, rich, and developed (WEIRD) countries, limiting our current understanding of identity development. Second, we focus on the topic of cultural identity development, an identity domain particularly relevant to immigrant and ethnic/racial minority youth.

Identity Development Across Cultural Context. A prevailing criticism of identity theory has been its focus on youth from WEIRD countries (Schwartz, Zamboanga, et al., 2012). This not only is unrepresentative of youth throughout the world but also has led to a focus on identity development from a largely individualistic perspective. Indeed, identity status theorists often adopt a pejorative view of foreclosure, despite the appropriateness of foreclosure in some cultural contexts marked by collectivism and an emphasis on conformity, hierarchical relationships, and interdependence (Dwairy, 2002). The consideration of various identity alternatives, which is viewed as a hallmark of "successful" identity development in many Western societies, may occur less frequently in non-Western societies (Schwartz, Zamboanga, et al., 2012). Indeed, prior studies have indicated that although commitment making may function similarly across East Asian and Western cultural contexts, exploration may not best represent the method by which youth construct their sense of self (Berman et al., 2011). In contrast, identity development in societies marked by collectivism may be more likely to include imitation and internalization of values and beliefs from parents and other authority figures (Cheng & Berman, 2012).

Cultural Identity Development. It is also important to note that identity development, as a result of systemic racism, ethnic/racial stratification, and xenophobia, is often more complex for immigrant and ethnic/racial minority youth compared with U.S.-born, ethnic majority youth (Syed & Mitchell, 2013). In addition to developing a general sense of personal identity, which is a normative developmental task, immigrant and ethnic/racial minority students are also confronted with the task of developing a cultural identity (Meca, Eichas, et al., 2019). Broadly, cultural identity refers to how individuals define themselves in relation to the cultural groups to which they belong (Schwartz et al., 2010). Although many constructs may fall under cultural identity, the two most widely studied components are ethnic/racial and U.S. identity (Meca et al., 2020).

Ethnic/racial identity (ERI) can be represented as a multidimensional construct encompassing individuals' beliefs and attitudes about their ethnicity and race as well as the process by which these beliefs and attitudes develop over time (Umaña-Taylor et al., 2014). Drawing on this conceptualization, U.S. identity has also been conceptualized to reflect individuals' beliefs and attitudes about their national group membership and the process by which these beliefs and attitudes develop over time (Schwartz, Park, et al., 2012). In operationalizing ERI and U.S. identity, research has largely turned to the ego identity perspective proposed in Phinney's (1989) ethnic identity model, which draws on Marcia's (1966) identity status paradigm and social identity theory (SIT; Tajfel, 1981).

Drawing on Marcia's (1966) operationalization of identity development, Phinney (1989) highlighted *exploration* and *commitment* as two key processes underlying cultural identity development. Cultural identity *exploration* refers to direct participation in events or experiences that teach individuals about the cultural groups to which they belong (e.g., attending social activities, participating in cultural traditions), talking to others, or thinking about one's ethnicity (Syed et al., 2013). On the other hand, cultural identity *commitment* refers to an understanding of what one's cultural group membership means to them (Schwartz et al., 2014). Drawing on SIT's (Tajfel, 1981) notion that individuals strive to achieve a positive social identity by adopting positive attitudes toward the groups to which they belong, Phinney (1989) identified a third component, *affirmation*, which refers to how an individual feels about their cultural group membership (Umaña-Taylor et al., 2004).

The value in cultural identity is strongly rooted in its capacity to promote positive psychosocial functioning. Conceptually, an understanding of the meaning of one's ethnicity and race answers the broader question "Who am I as a member of my group?" (Meca et al., 2017), which serves to provide youth with a sense of confidence that reinforces convictions regarding the meaning of their ethnicity and nationality in their lives. In the absence of a strong cultural identity, individuals may lack direction regarding how to proceed when they encounter situations that are inconsistent with their experiences (Schwartz et al., 2006). Consistently, research has explored the links between ERI and U.S. identity with psychosocial functioning broadly. In a comprehensive review, Rivas-Drake et al. (2014) documented the extensive body of research linking ERI and well-being and internalizing problem behaviors across ethnic/racial groups. Although some studies indicated null findings, as a whole, commitment and affirmation were positively and differentially associated with psychosocial adjustment. Moreover, recent research suggests that ERI can reduce the negative effects of discrimination. For example, Kogan et al. (2014) found that ERI mediated the association between discrimination and depressive symptoms among African Americans.

Research on U.S. identity has been less prevalent within the literature; however, Meca et al. (2020) recently explored the links between ERI and U.S. affirmation, commitment, and exploration with well-being, self-esteem, and depression among Latinx youth. ERI affirmation and commitment were positively associated with well-being and self-esteem and negatively associated with depressive symptoms. In contrast, although U.S. identity was not associated with either well-being or self-esteem, it was negatively associated with depressive symptoms. As a whole, these findings indicate that the establishment of an ERI and a U.S. identity serves as a source of strength for immigrant and ethnic/racial minority students (Meca et al., 2020; Rivas-Drake et al., 2014). The transition from an industrial to a technological society has resulted in drastic changes in the lives of college students. Today, the transition to adulthood is more individually directed and less socially prescribed (Schwartz et al., 2005)—placing the burden on students to navigate an overwhelming, unstructured period. With proper support, we can facilitate positive identity development.

Guiding Questions

1. How might I provide opportunities to critically reflect on existing identity choices, encouraging self-discovery and self-construction?
2. How can I encourage my students to explore a breadth of fields to ensure their existing goals are aligned with their potentials?
3. How can I build supportive relationships with my students that foster autonomy and individuality while navigating timelines and graduation expectations?
4. How can my own biases and privilege impact my ideas of what are appropriate or adequate identity decisions? What are some ways I can support positive identity development in emerging adults?

References

American College Health Association. (2018). American College Health Association-National College Health Assessment II: Reference Group Executive Summary Fall 2017. https://www.acha.org/documents/ncha/NCHA-II_FALL_2017_REFERENCE_GROUP_EXECUTIVE_SUMMARY.pdf

Arango, L. L., Kurtines, W. M., Montgomery, M. J., & Ritchie, R. (2008). A multi-stage longitudinal comparative design stage II evaluation of the Changing Lives Program: The Life

Course Interview (RDA-LCI). *Journal of Adolescent Research, 23*(3), 310–341. https://doi.org/10.1177/0743558408314381

Arnett, J. J. (2000). Emerging adulthood: A theory of development from the late teens through the twenties. *American Psychologist, 55*(5), 469–480. https://doi.org/10.1037/0003-066X.55.5.469

Arnett, J. J. (2007). Emerging adulthood: What is it, and what is it good for? *Child Development Perspectives, 1*(2), 68–73. https://doi.org/10.1111/j.1750-8606.2007.00016.x

Baumeister, R. F., & Leary, M. R. (1995). The need to belong: Desire for interpersonal attachments as a fundamental human motivation. *Psychological Bulletin, 117*(3), 497–529. https://doi.org/10.1037/0033-2909.117.3.497

Berman, S. L., You, Y. F., Schwartz, S., Teo, G., & Mochizuki, K. (2011). Identity exploration, commitment, and distress: A cross national investigation in China, Taiwan, Japan, and the United States. *Child Youth Care Forum, 40*(1), 65–75. https://doi.org/10.1007/s10566-010-9127-1

Berzonsky, M. D. (2016). An exploration of personal assumptions about self-construction and self-discovery. *Identity: An International Journal of Theory and Research, 16*(4), 267–281. https://doi.org/10.1080/15283488.2016.1229609

Berzonsky, M. D., & Neimeyer, G. J. (1994). Ego identity status and identity processing orientation: The moderating role of commitment. *Journal of Research in Personality, 28*(4), 425–435. https://doi.org/10.1006/jrpe.1994.1030

Carlone, H. B., & Johnson, A. (2007). Understanding the science experiences of women of color: Science identity as an analytic lens. *Journal of Research in Science Teaching, 44*(8), 1187–1218. https://doi-org.proxy.lib.odu.edu/10.1002/tea.20237

Center for Collegiate Mental Health. (2020, January). 2019 Annual Report (Publication No. STA 20-244).

Cheng, M., & Berman, S. L. (2012). Globalization and identity development: A Chinese perspective. In S. J. Schwartz (Ed.), *New directions for child and adolescent development: Vol. 2012. Identity around the world* (pp. 103–121). Jossey-Bass/Wiley.

Côté, J. E. (2019). *Youth development in identity societies: Paradoxes of purpose.* Routledge.

Crocetti, E., Klimstra, T., Keijsers, L., Hale, W. W., & Meeus, W. (2009). Anxiety trajectories and identity development in adolescence: A five-wave longitudinal study. *Journal of Youth and Adolescence, 38*(6), 839–849. https://doi.org/10.1007/s10964-008-9302-y

Crocetti, E., Luyckx, K., Scrignaro, M., & Sica, L. S. (2011). Identity formation in Italian emerging adults: A cluster-analytic approach and associations with psychosocial functioning. *European Journal of Developmental Psychology, 8*(5), 558–572. https://doi.org/10.1080/17405629.2011.576858

Dwairy, M. (2002). Foundations of psychosocial dynamic personality theory of collective people. *Clinical Psychology Review, 22*(3), 343–360. https://doi.org/10.1016/S0272-7358(01)00100-3

Eichas, K., Meca, A., Montgomery, M., & Kurtines, W. M. (2014). Identity and positive youth development: Advances in developmental intervention science. In K. McLean & M. Syed (Eds.), *Oxford handbook of identity development* (pp. 337–354). Oxford University Press.

Eichas, K., Montgomery, M. J., Meca, A., & Kurtines, W. M. (2017). Empowering marginalized youth: A self-transformative intervention for promoting positive youth development. *Child Development, 88*(4), 1115–1124. https://doi-org.proxy.lib.odu.edu/10.1111/cdev.12866

Erikson, E. H. (1968). *Identity: Youth and crisis.* Norton.

Hihara, S., Sugimura, K., & Syed, M. (2018). Forming a negative identity in contemporary society: Shedding light on the most problematic identity resolution. *Identity, 18*(4), 325–333. https://doi.org/10.1080/15283488.2018.1524329

Hofstede, G. (2015). The Hofstede Centre: Strategy, Culture, Change. http://geert-hofstede.com/countries.html

Kitzrow, M. A. (2003). The mental health needs of today's college students: Challenges and recommendations. *Journal of Student Affairs Research and Practice, 41*(1), 167–181.

Koepke, S., & Denissen, J. J. (2012). Dynamics of identity development and separation-individuation in parent-child relationships during adolescence and emerging adulthood: A conceptual integration. *Developmental Review, 32*(1), 67–88. https://doi.org/10.1016/j.dr.2012.01.001

Kogan, S. M., Yu, T., Allen, K. A., & Brody, G. H. (2014). Racial microstressors, racial self-concept, and depressive symptoms among male African Americans during the transition to adulthood. *Journal of Youth and Adolescence, 44*(4), 898–909. https://doi.org/10.1007/s10964-014-0199-3

Kroger, J., & Marcia, J. E. (2011). The identity statuses: Origins, meanings, and interpretations. In S. J. Schwartz, K. Luyckx, & V. L. Vignoles (Eds.), *Handbook of identity theory and research* (pp. 31–53). Springer.

Luyckx, K., Schwartz, S. J., Berzonsky, M. D., Soenens, B., Vansteenkiste, M., Smits, I., & Goossens, L. (2008). Capturing ruminative exploration: Extending the four-dimensional model of identity formation in late adolescence. *Journal of Research in Personality, 42*(1), 58–82. https://doi.org/10.1016/j.jrp.2007.04.004

Marcia, J. E. (1966). Development and validation of ego-identity status. *Journal of Personal and Social Psychology, 3*(5), 551–558. https://doi.org/10.1037/h0023281

Meca, A., Eichas, K., Quintana, S., Maximin, B. M., Ritchie, R. A., Madrazo, V. L., Harari, G. M., & Kurtines, W. M. (2014). Reducing identity distress: Results of an identity intervention for emerging adults. *Identity: An International Journal of Theory of Research, 14*, 312–331. https://doi.org/10.1080/15283488.2014.944696

Meca, A., Eichas, K., Schwartz, S. J., & Davis, R. (2019). Biculturalism and bicultural identity development: A relational model of bicultural systems. In P. F. Titzmann & P. Jugert (Eds.), *Youth in superdiverse societies: Growing up with globalization, diversity, and acculturation* (pp. 41–57). Routledge/Psychology Press.

Meca, A., Gonzales-Backen, M., Davis, R., Hassell, T., & Rodil, J. (2020). Development of the United States Identity Scale: Unpacking affirmation and commitment. *Journal of Latinx Psychology, 8*, 127–141. doi:10.1037/lat0000135

Meca, A., Rodil, J. C., Paulson, J. F., Kelley, M., Schwartz, S. J., Unger, J. B., Lorenzo-Blanco, E. I., Des Rosiers, S. E., Gonzales-Backen, M., Baezconde-Garbanati, L., & Zamboanga, B. L. (2019). Examining the directionality between identity development and depressive symptoms among recently immigrated Hispanic adolescents. *Journal of Youth and Adolescence, 48*, 2114–2124. https://doi.org/10.1007/s10964-019-01086-z

Meca, A., Sabet, R. F., Farrelly, C. M., Benitez, C. G., Schwartz, S. J., Gonzales-Backen, M., Lorenzo-Blanco, E. I., Unger, J. B., Zamboanga, B. L., Baezconde-Garbanati, L., Picariello, S., Des Rosiers, S. E., Soto, D. W., Pattarroyo, M., Villamar, J. A., & Lizzi, K. M. (2017). Personal and cultural identity development in recently immigrated Hispanic adolescents: Links with psychosocial functioning. *Cultural Diversity and Ethnic Minority Psychology, 23*(3), 348–361. https://doi.org/10.1037/cdp0000129

Phinney, J. S. (1989). Stages of ethnic identity in minority group adolescents. *Journal of Early Adolescence, 9*, 34–49. http://dx.doi.org/10.1177/0272431689091004

Ritchie, R. A., Meca, A., Madrazo, V. L., Schwartz, S. J., Hardy, S. A., Zamboanga, B. L., Weisskirch, R. S., Kim, S. Y., Whitbourne, S. K., Ham, L. S., & Lee, R. M. (2013). Identity dimensions and related processes in emerging adulthood: Helpful or harmful? *Journal of Clinical Psychology, 69*, 415–432. doi:10.1002/jclp.21960

Rivas-Drake, D., Seaton, E. K., Markstrom, C., Quintana, S., Syed, M., Lee, R. M., Schwartz, S. J., Umaña-Taylor, A. J., French, S., & Yip, T. (2014). Ethnic and racial identity in adolescence: Implications for psychosocial, academic, and health outcomes. *Child Development, 85*(1), 40–57. https://doi.org/10.1111/cdev.12200

Schwartz, S. J. (2016). Turning point for a turning point: Advancing emerging adulthood theory and research. *Emerging Adulthood, 4*(5), 307–317. https://doi.org/10.1177/2167696815624640

Schwartz, S. J., Beters, W., Luyckx, K., Soenens, B., Zamboanga, B. L., Forthun, L. F., Hardy, S. A., Vazsonyi, A. T., Ham, L. S., Kim, S. Y., Whitbourne, S. K., & Waterman, A. S. (2011). Examining the light and dark sides of emerging adults' identity: A study of identity status differences in positive and negative psychosocial functioning. *Journal of Youth and Adolescence, 40*, 839–859. https://doi.org/10.1007/s10964-010-9606-6

Schwartz, S. J., Côté, J. E., & Arnett, J. J. (2005). Identity and agency in emerging adulthood: Two developmental routes in the individualization process. *Youth & Society, 37*(2), 201–229.

Schwartz, S. J., Montgomery, M. J., & Briones, E. (2006). The role of identity in acculturation among immigrant people: Theoretical propositions, empirical questions, and applied recommendations. *Human Development, 49*, 1–30. http://dx.doi.org/10.1159/000090300

Schwartz, S. J., Park, I. J. K., Huynh, Q., Zamboanga, B. L., Umaña-Taylor, A. J., Lee, R. M., Rodriguez, L., Kim, S. Y., Whitbourne, S. K., Castillo, L. G., Weisskirch, R. S., Vazsonyi, A. T., Williams, M. K., & Agocha, V. B. (2012). The American identity measure: Development and validation across ethnic group and immigrant generation. *Identity: An International Journal of Theory and Research, 12*, 93–128. http://dx.doi.org/10.1080/15283488.2012.668730

Schwartz, S. J., Syed, M., Yip, T., Knight, G. P., Umaña-Taylor, A. J., Rivas-Drake, D., & Lee, R. M. (2014). Methodological issues in ethnic and racial identity research with ethnic minority populations: Theoretical precision, measurement issues, and research designs. *Child Development, 85*, 58–76. http://dx.doi.org/10.1111/cdev.12201

Schwartz, S. J., Unger, J. B., Zamboanga, B. L., & Szapocznik, J. (2010). Rethinking the concept of acculturation: Implications for theory and research. *American Psychologist, 65*, 237–251. http://dx.doi.org/10.1037/a0019330

Schwartz, S. J., Zamboanga, B. L., Luyckx, K., Meca, A., & Ritchie, R. A. (2015). Identity in emerging adulthood: Reviewing the field and looking forward. In J. J. Arnett (Ed.), *The Oxford handbook of emerging adulthood* (pp. 401–420). Oxford University Press.

Schwartz, S. J., Zamboanga, B. L., Meca, A., & Ritchie, R. A. (2012). Identity around the world: An overview. In S. J. Schwartz (Ed.), *New directions for child and adolescent development: Vol. 2012. Identity around the world* (pp. 1–18). Jossey-Bass/Wiley.

Schwartz, S. J., Zamboanga, B. L., Weisskirch, R. S., & Rodriguez, L. (2009). The relationships of personal and ethnic identity exploration to indices of adaptive and maladaptive psychosocial functioning. *International Journal of Behavioral Development, 33*(2), 131–144. https://doi.org/10.1177/0165025408098018

Syed, M., & Mitchell, L. L. (2013). Race, ethnicity, and emerging adulthood: Retrospect and prospects. *Emerging Adulthood, 1*(2), 83–95. https://doi.org/10.1177/2167696813480503

Syed, M., Walker, L. H. M., Lee, R. M., Umaña-Taylor, A. J., Zamboanga, B. L., Schwartz, S. J., Armenta, B. E., & Huynh, Q.-L. (2013). A two-factor model of ethnic identity exploration: Implications for identity coherence and well-being. *Cultural Diversity and Ethnic Minority Psychology, 19*(2), 143–154. https://doi.org/10.1037/a0030564

Tajfel, H. (1981). *Human groups and social categories: Studies in social psychology*. Cambridge University Press.

Umaña-Taylor, A. J., Quintana, S. M., Lee, R. M., Cross, W. E., Jr., Rivas-Drake, D., Schwartz, S. J., Syed, M., Yip, T., Seaton, E., & Ethnic and Racial Identity in the 21st Century Study Group. (2014). Ethnic and racial identity revisited: An integrated conceptualization. *Child Development, 85*, 21–39. http://dx.doi.org/10.1111/cdev.12196

Umaña-Taylor, A. J., Yazedjian, A., & Bámaca-Gómez, M. Y. (2004). Developing the ethnic identity scale using Eriksonian and social identity perspectives. *Identity: An International Journal of Theory and Research, 4,* 9–38. http://dx.doi.org/10.1207/S1532706XID0401_2

Waterman, A. S., Schwartz, S. J., Hardy, S. A., Kim, S. Y., Lee, R. M., Armenta, B. E., Whitbourne, S. K., Zamboanga, B. L.; Brown, E. J., Williams, M. K., & Agocha, V. B. (2013). Good choices, poor choices: Relationship between the quality of identity commitments and psychosocial functioning. *Emerging Adulthood, 1*(3), 163–174. https://doi.org/10.1177/2167696813484004

3

"We Got In!"

The Influence and Role of Family on Relationships and Decision-Making

Kayla Reed-Fitzke and Elizabeth R. Watters

The transition to college is often celebrated as a child's first step into adulthood. Although emerging adults are at the age of majority and legally adults in the United States, they remain an important part of the child subsystem within their family of origin. As emerging adults begin the process of differentiating, or separating, from their families, they may face ambiguity regarding how they define new roles and identities as a newfound adult while still "children" within their family. How emerging adults and their families renegotiate their relationship dynamics, boundaries, and expectations is linked to an emerging adult's ability to successfully navigate the biopsychosocial, financial, and academic transition to higher education.

This chapter focuses on the continued importance and impact of the family, particularly parental figures, during this transitional life period. We refer to parents and all other parental figures as parents throughout the chapter. We will provide a brief overview of seminal interdisciplinary theories to situate the importance of the family during this period. We will also discuss two contrasting sets of parental behaviors (i.e., helicopter parenting and autonomy-supportive parenting) and their consequences, as well as the myriad ways parental involvement shapes the collegiate experience. Next, we highlight varying experiences in two unique subsets of emerging adults—first-generation students and those who lack parental support. We then pull together many of the discussed facets in a case study with questions to apply the content to a real case. We close with general suggestions for working with emerging adults in higher education.

Kayla Reed-Fitzke and Elizabeth R. Watters, *"We Got In!"* In: *Cultivating Student Success.* Edited by: Tisha A. Duncan and Allison A. Buskirk-Cohen, Oxford University Press. © Oxford University Press 2022. DOI: 10.1093/oso/9780197586693.003.0004

Family Systems Theory and Adult Attachment

Family systems theory and attachment theory both center on family processes, specifically by viewing relationships and families as systems (Rothbaum et al., 2002). Family systems theory attends to how family dynamics, structures, roles, communication, boundaries, and power differentials influence family functioning (Bowen, 1978; Rothbaum et al., 2002). From this perspective, families are emotional systems, which can be made up of parental and child subsystems (Bowen, 1978). During transitions, families renegotiate their system (e.g., roles, interactions) and the boundaries within it (Bowen, 1978). A central facet of this theory rests on the importance of gaining (or maintaining) differentiation (i.e., balancing autonomy and connectedness) from one's family of origin (Bowen, 1978). Well-differentiated individuals are able to make decisions independently while maintaining appropriate emotional connections (Bowen, 1978; Carter & McGoldrick, 1989). Becoming well differentiated is a salient process in emerging adulthood. Problems during emerging adulthood and the transition to higher education may arise if families have issues renegotiating their relationships and differentiating.

Attachment theory builds upon the core tenet that the parent-child relationship is a base from which children explore their identity and environment; a safe, consistent base (i.e., secure attachment) provides the foundation for how to build successful relationships (Bowlby, 2008). Although this base is formed in infancy, parental support and secure parent-child attachment continues to be important well into emerging adulthood. A parent-child relationship that is characterized by support and secure attachment helps promote healthy and adaptive coping during stressful periods (Cutrona et al., 1994; Mattanah et al., 2011) and can act as a protective mechanism against negative psychosocial outcomes (Kahn et al., 2017; Love, 2008). A secure parental attachment provides the basis upon which students navigate social and academic transitions (Cutrona et al., 1994; Fass & Tubman, 2002; Melendez & Melendez, 2010), which are critical in promoting emerging adults' ability to succeed during their transition to college.

The Self-Determination Theory

The self-determination theory (SDT) is a framework commonly used to understand and promote motivation and well-being. SDT also provides a lens through which the role of parent-child relationships in emerging adulthood can be understood. A central proposition of SDT is that individuals have three basic psychological needs that are necessary for health, well-being, and development (Deci & Ryan, 1985; Ryan & Deci, 2002). These three needs are autonomy (i.e., sense of control in one's decisions and behavior), competence (i.e., confidence one's actions will achieve a desired outcome), and relatedness (i.e., caring for, and feeling cared for by, important others; Deci & Ryan, 2000; Ryan & Deci, 2002). These needs are supported (or thwarted) by the multiple environments (e.g., family, school, peer) in which individuals exist (Deci & Ryan, 2000; Ryan & Deci, 2002). As such, the family environment can promote the well-being and healthy development of emerging adults by supporting their psychological needs.

Additionally, each individual relationship within a larger environment can provide a sense of relatedness. To do so, individuals must support the autonomy and competence of the other in the relationship (Deci & Ryan, 2014). This notion aligns nicely with the family system perspective, in that a key developmental task of emerging adulthood centers on gaining independence and competence while maintaining healthy emotional connections with their parents (i.e., differentiation). Through the lens of SDT, both the larger family environment and the individual relationships within that family system serve to support (or hinder) the development of emerging adults by supporting (or thwarting) their psychological needs.

Helicopter Parenting

The term "helicopter parenting" is largely attributed to Cline and Fay (1990), who used the term as a metaphor for parents who hover over their children and rescue them when challenges arise. Helicopter parenting is commonly used to refer to parents who not only hover but also are overly involved/micromanage daily activities, make decisions for their child, and try to protect them from experiencing failure and making mistakes (e.g., Locke et al., 2012). In general, helicopter parenting is marked by developmentally inappropriate behavioral control and autonomy limiting but is distinct from psychological control (Padilla-Walker & Nelson, 2012). Terms including "bulldozer," "lawnmower," and "curling parents" in Scandinavia, and "little emperor syndrome" and "tiger mom" in China, have been used to describe these overparenting behaviors. For the purposes of the present chapter, we will use the term "helicopter parenting" as an umbrella term for the various types of intrusive, overparenting behaviors.

There have been several historical and societal changes over the last several decades that may have contributed to the rise in, or increased attention to, helicopter parenting. A shift in societal expectations of parents took place over the second half of the last century. Parents are expected to be involved in their child's lives more now than ever before. Between the 1970s and 2005, the amount of time parents spent with their children had increased by approximately 6 hours each week (Hamermesh et al., 2005). There have also been increasing expectations regarding attendance in formal education around the world (U.S. Department of Education, Institute of Education Sciences, National Center for Education Statistics, 2016). Pairing such expectations with economic recessions and rising inequality results in a hypercompetitive admission process and job market. Given that parents are expected to be more involved, parents feel a heightened sense of pressure to set their children up for academic success. Advances in technology also facilitate helicopter parenting by providing parents a means to being overly involved. Parents increasingly communicate with their adult children via text and social media (Sarigiani et al., 2013; Stein et al., 2016); the majority of parents communicate with their collegiate emerging adults between a couple times a week and multiple times a day (Reed, 2017).

Helicopter parenting has been linked to myriad negative consequences, such as emotional and behavioral problems (Cui et al., 2019; Schiffrin et al., 2014; Segrin et al., 2015), lower self-worth (Nelson et al., 2015), lower self-efficacy (Reed et al., 2016; van Ingen et al., 2015), ineffective coping skills (Segrin et al., 2013), lower life satisfaction (Schiffrin et al., 2014), alienation from peers (van Ingen et al., 2015), and narcissism (Segrin et al., 2013). Emerging adults with helicopter parents have been described as overly needy (i.e., seeking attention, approval, and direction; Odenweller et al., 2014). Such parenting behaviors may not always overtly work to reduce emerging adult well-being but may indirectly do so by reducing one's psychological needs (e.g., Reed et al., 2016; Schiffrin et al., 2014). There is also evidence that helicopter parenting may be more harmful in certain contexts. For example, such behaviors may have a worse impact when not accompanied by parental warmth (Nelson et al., 2015). The impact of helicopter parenting can also vary based on cultural norms and expectations of parents and their children (Bornstein, 2012). Although the research examining cultural variation is limited, there does appear to be a differential impact across culture, albeit there are more similarities than differences (Pinquart & Kauser, 2018). The nuanced variations across culture have only just begun to be compared, but the differences appear to mainly lie in the perception of parenting behaviors across Western and non-Western cultures.

As an individual working with emerging adults in higher education, it is important to note that such parenting behaviors also can positively impact emerging adults. Many parents do not believe such overcontrol is connected to negative outcomes (Segrin et al., 2015); often the intent of helicopter parents is not to overcontrol, but rather to help their child(ren) be successful. Helicopter parenting has been linked to an increased perception of parental emotional support (Padilla-Walker & Nelson, 2012), greater physical health (Reed et al., 2016), and positive family outcomes (e.g., openness, guidance; Padilla-Walker & Nelson, 2012). Emerging adults with highly involved parents also tend to report more interaction with teachers, greater educational gains, and more general satisfaction with their collegiate experience (Shoup et al., 2009).

Although the media and anecdotal stories from those in education paint helicopter parenting as pervasive and inherently problematic, the reality is that most parents provide an appropriate level of support and engage in developmentally appropriate relationships (e.g., Lowe et al., 2015; Luyckx et al., 2007; Urry et al., 2011). The majority of emerging adults have parents who do not engage in extreme overparenting behaviors. However, we recognize such realities do not deter from the fact that working with emerging adults who have more "extreme" helicopter parents can be especially challenging. We will revisit this concept again in the case study at the close of this chapter.

Developmentally Appropriate and Autonomy-Supportive Parenting

Many of the challenges that arise with parenting during emerging adulthood and the transition to college center on the extent to which parents are involved. In contrast to helicopter parenting, autonomy-supportive parenting refers to parenting behaviors that are based on a developmentally appropriate level of involvement. Specifically, autonomy-supportive parents are those who continue to have an active and involved role in their child's life while being mindful of their child's perspective and encouraging their ability to solve their own problems (Deci & Ryan, 2000; Grolnick et al., 1991). Such age-appropriate parenting promotes healthy differentiation as family dynamics shift during this developmental period (Bowen, 1978; Rothbaum et al., 2002). Although developmentally appropriate and autonomy-supportive parenting has been less extensively examined in the context of emerging adulthood, we do know it is linked to positive outcomes. For example, parent–emerging adult child relationships characterized by warmth, connection, and minimal control tend to foster emerging adult competence (Lindell et al., 2017) and have been linked with better mental health and internal concepts (Liem et al., 2010; Nelson et al., 2015; Reed et al., 2016).

Developmentally appropriate parenting is characterized by decreased monitoring of behaviors; less rule setting and enforcement; decreased inhibiting of emerging adult self-expression, opinions, and perspectives; and increased support of autonomy and decision-making (Lindell et al., 2017), which in turn promotes competency and decision-making abilities (Bradley-Giest & Olson-Buchanan, 2014). This increased individuality and competency is then linked with successful adjustment to college and greater overall satisfaction with university life (Mattanah et al., 2004; Pedersen, 2017). Understanding these developmental needs of emerging adult families has direct implications for those working in higher education settings who have the opportunity to support autonomy and boundaries between students and families, provide psychoeducation, and normalize the stressors related to leaving home.

Parental Involvement and Its Impact on the Collegiate Experience

Parents can influence students' college choice, major, and career trajectory (Dennis et al., 2005; Nichols & Islas, 2016; Renzulli & Barr, 2017; Workman, 2015). This is especially true for families who provide a strong financial incentive and support to attend college (Flaster, 2018, 2020; Hamilton, 2013; Lowe & Arnett, 2020; Padilla-Walker et al., 2012). This begins prior to even choosing what colleges to apply to, as emerging adults with parents who are willing/able to provide financial aid are more likely to apply for college (Flaster, 2018, 2020). Financial stressors may influence both the parents' and emerging adults' expectations for attending college, which may be especially true for middle-class families compared to lower-class families (Lowe & Arnett, 2020; Renzulli & Barr, 2017). After receiving admission, in comparison to lower socioeconomic groups, parents from higher, more affluent socioeconomic groups provide their emerging adult students with greater academic, social, and career support, as well as access to exclusive university infrastructure, because of their ability to provide greater financial incentives and access to social capital (Hamilton et al., 2015). Although parental financial aid has been linked to lower grade point averages (GPAs), it has been linked to higher graduation rates (Hamilton, 2013).

In addition to financial support, parental emotional support also impacts emerging adults' daily experiences (e.g., schoolwork, friendships, romantic relationships). However, such impact likely depends on the level of detail emerging adults share with their parents. Emerging adults, in general, continue to share information with their parents, with students often soliciting support from their parents (Pizzolato & Hicklen, 2011). Common areas in which emerging adults seek advice from their parents are work-life balance, academic concerns, social and relational concerns, financial concerns, and current job or future career concerns (Carlson, 2014). Parental emotional support can also impact emerging adult collegiate success in more subtle ways. For example, parental involvement and parent-child attachment both work to build up positive self-concepts (e.g., self-esteem, self-efficacy), which in turn influence educational outcomes (Causey et al., 2015; Holt, 2014; Thompson & Verdino, 2019; Yuan et al., 2016).

Parental involvement may be of particular importance for students who identify as Black, Indigenous, and People of Color (BIPOC), as such students often face additional stressors during this transition. Secure parent-child attachment can provide BIPOC students with an increased sense of security as they navigate such stressors (e.g., racial disparities, discrimination; Melendez & Melendez, 2010). The importance of parental support also may vary across larger cultural values, such as between collectivism and individualism. For example, self-efficacy is more influenced by and dependent on parent-child relationships for students from more collectivistic cultures, which emphasize support and intimacy (e.g., Asian American, African American), compared to students from more individualist cultures (e.g., European American; Yuan et al., 2016).

What About First-Generation Students?

Several decades' worth of evidence tells us first-generation (first-gen) students have a different experience than continuing-generation students (Covarrubias & Fryberg, 2015; Lindell et al., 2017; London, 1989). While continuing-generation students benefit from their family's experience in higher education, such as having access to greater social capital, higher entitlement, greater confidence in their academic abilities, and knowledge about college norms/expectations, which increases their tendency to seek help and critique classes/professors (Nichols & Islas, 2016), college is new territory for the entire first-generation family. The parents themselves experience additional transitional stressors, which influence how they communicate and navigate changes in family dynamics, as well as engagement with the university (Harper et al., 2020). Although parents may be unsure how to help their student navigate college, they tend to have higher levels of interaction with their students and a greater desire for more engagement with their student's college (Reed, 2017). As a result, these parents may be more prone to enacting behavioral control, psychological control, and helicopter parenting behavior, which may cause the emerging adult to feel that they have a responsibility to act as a "delegate" for the family (Lindell et al., 2017; London, 1989).

Additionally, first-generation students are more likely to identify as BIPOC and come from lower socioeconomic backgrounds than continuing generation students (Blackwell & Pinder, 2014; Hartig & Steigerwald, 2007). BIPOC parents may fear their children will lose their cultural identities (Hartig & Steigerwald, 2007), especially as their students confront cultural discrepancies between their family values and university experiences (Covarrubias et al., 2019). Such students may also experience "family achievement guilt," or guilt related to their opportunity to attend college and break away from their families and home environment (Covarrubias & Fryberg, 2015). However, BIPOC first-generation students may view college as necessary for survival and a way to break free of intergenerational cycles, which may drive internal motivation to reach academic goals regardless of the additional barriers they may face (Blackwell & Pinder, 2014). For those working in higher education settings, it is important to have nuanced resources in place to help first-generation and underrepresented students and their families navigate their unique questions, concerns, and stressors when navigating this transition.

What About Students Who Lack Parental Support or Involvement?

We would be remiss if we did not acknowledge that many college students may come from an adverse family environment and do not have, or want, familial support. An estimated 61% of the population has experienced one or more adverse childhood experiences (ACEs; e.g., poverty or financial insecurity, abuse) between the ages of 0 and 17 (Division of Violence Prevention, 2019), indicating that many emerging adults you interact with have experienced some type of traumatic event prior to college, which may impact their overall development and adjustment (Hinojosa et al., 2018; Mitchell & Abraham, 2018). The negative effects of ACEs may be particularly exacerbated for low-income, urban, BIPOC emerging adults who have cumulative trauma (i.e., two or more ACEs; Mersky et al., 2013). Emerging adults who lack parental support when transitioning to higher education are more likely to experience poor outcomes, such as loneliness, which may put individuals at risk for anxiety and depression (Mounts et al., 2006). While research is still needed to understand the intersection of adverse home environments, lack of parental support and involvement, and emerging adults' transition to college, it is clear that students who face childhood adversity and lack parental support face additional barriers.

For students who do not have familial support, social support from peers may be particularly critical. Even among those who do have supportive parents, students begin to shift their attachment from parental figures to peers during late adolescence and emerging adulthood (Dennis et al., 2005; Fass & Tubman, 2002). Peer attachment, friendship quality, a sense of belonging, and general peer social support have been linked to increased competency, acceptance, self-worth, self-esteem, optimism, and decreased internalizing and externalizing behaviors (Duncan et al., 2019; Fass & Tubman, 2002; Pittman & Richmond, 2008). Individuals transitioning to college often have more challenges adjusting if they do not have a strong, supportive network (Brissette et al., 2002). Peer support is especially important for first-generation and BIPOC students, as it has been linked to both academic (e.g., cumulative GPA, adjustment, commitment; Dennis et al., 2005) and personal factors (e.g., reduced suicidal risk; Thomas & Brausch, 2020). Peer support has a critical role, in that it may in part offset some of the challenges faced by first-generation and BIPOC students' families (e.g., limited level of knowledge vs. continuing generation students, systemic barriers to success, adverse family environments; Nichols & Islas, 2016; Reed et al., 2015). Students with peer support receive additional help, guidance, and emotional support, which can help to normalize some of the transitional stressors they face and facilitate adjustment (Dennis et al., 2005; Thomas & Brausch, 2020).

Case Study

Ellison (they/them/their) is a 21-year-old, Asian American, gender nonbinary individual from the rural Midwest. They are about to enter their junior year, majoring in gender studies. They struggled over the first two years as a first-generation college student.

Ellison works part time at the library and tutors students to cover their bills and daily expenses. Ellison's parents have full access to their bank account and their mother receives monthly bank statements, which she reviews and then texts Ellison about when there are "concerning" transactions. Ellison feels compelled to Venmo (i.e., electronically transfer money) their best friend anytime they want to buy something and does not want their parents to know. Even though Ellison's parents do not pay their tuition or bills, they worry their parents will be personally offended and mistrust them if they try setting boundaries regarding their finances.

Ellison's parents believe their choice of major was not a good decision and have contacted their academic advisor with questions about how to switch majors. Ellison has tried to explain that they plan to go to graduate school; however, their parents are not supportive as it will cost more money. Although they have been financially independent over the past two years and have received undergraduate research scholarships, their parents worry they are not working hard enough as the results do not seem as tangible to them. This has resulted in ongoing conflict and relational tension as Ellison tries to explain their work and why receiving a B will not prevent them from doing well in grad school.

Ellison also has a hard time with how their parents view their gender identity and sexuality. Prior to coming out to their parents, Ellison's mother used to ask them questions about their interest in dating and would give them relationship advice. Now, when Ellison tries to talk about dating relationships, their mother makes negative comments about their gender orientation, pronouns, and sexuality and how this is just a phase. Such responses trigger memories of Ellison's childhood, when their mother was emotionally abusive. This pattern of thinking tends to spiral into remembering the periods in which their family lived in poverty, when they were bullied during middle and high school, and the discrimination they faced in their community and church after they came out as queer.

Their mom and aunt decided to drive to campus and confront Ellison, speak with their academic and financial advisors, and try to convince them to move back home and attend community college. Ellison knows they do not want to move back home because they have been able to make several close friends and feel their gender and sexual identity is fully supported at their university. They also love their major and the work that they are doing. However, they feel conflicted over the decision because they want to make their parents happy, want to be respectful of their opinions, and do not want to cause additional stress or conflict for the family.

Guiding Questions

Please consider these questions given the capacity in which you work with emerging adults in higher education. Imagine that you have been contacted by a concerned professor (or are the professor).

1. What policies might you need to consult before taking any additional steps?

2. Aside from Ellison, who else might you collaborate with on this case? Who would you not want to involve?
3. What supports might you suggest Ellison use?
4. How can (insert your title here) work within the higher education system to help promote Ellison's well-being?
5. Would you consider Ellison's parents to be helicopter parents?
6. How does the family's boundaries and behaviors influence Ellison's health and transition to college?
7. How can Ellison and their family lean into this normal developmental period to better help Ellison have room to be an emerging adult?

References

Blackwell, E., & Pinder, P. (2014). What are the motivational factors of first-generation minority college students who overcome their family histories to pursue higher education? *College Student Journal, 48*(1), 45–56.

Bornstein, M. H. (2012). Cultural approaches to parenting. *Parenting, 12*, 212–221. https://doi.org/10.1080/15295192.2012.683359

Bowen, M. (1978). *Family therapy in clinical practice*. Aronson.

Bowlby, J. (2008). *A secure base: Parent-child attachment and healthy human development*. Basic Books.

Bradley-Giest, J. C., & Olson-Buchanan, J. B. (2014). Helicopter parents: An examination of the correlates of over-parenting of college students. *Education and Training, 54*, 314–328.

Brissette, I., Scheier, M. F., & Carver, C. S. (2002). The role of optimism in social network development, coping, and psycho- logical adjustment during a life transition. *Journal of Personality and Social Psychology, 82*, 102–111. https://doi.org/10.1037/0022-3514.82.1.102

Carlson, C. L. (2014). Seeking self-sufficiency: Why emerging adult college students receive and implement parental advice. *Emerging Adulthood, 2*, 257–269. https://doi.org/10.1177/2167696814551785

Carter, B., & McGoldrick, M. (1989). *The changing family life cycle: A framework for family therapy* (2nd ed.). Allyn and Bacon.

Causey, S., Livingston, J., & High, B. (2015). Family structure, racial socialization, perceived parental involvement, and social support as predictors of self-esteem in African American college students. *Journal of Black Studies, 46*(7), 655–677. https://doi.org/10.1177/0021934715592601

Cline, F. W., & Fay, J. (1990). *Parenting with love and logic: Teaching children responsibility*. Pinon Press.

Covarrubias, R., & Fryberg, S. (2015). Movin' on up (to college): First-generation college students' experiences with family achievement guilt. *Cultural Diversity and Ethnic Minority Psychology, 21*(3), 420–429. https://doi.org/10.1037/a0037844

Covarrubias, R., Valle, I., Laiduc, G., & Azmitia, M. (2019). "You never become fully independent": Family roles and independence in first-generation college students. *Journal of Adolescent Research, 34*(4), 381–410. https://doi.org/10.1177/0743558418788402

Cui, M., Graber, J., Metz, A., & Darling, C. (2019). Parental indulgence, self-regulation, and young adults' behavioral and emotional problems. *Journal of Family Studies, 25*, 233–249. https://doi.org/10.1080/13229400.2016.1237884

Cutrona, C. E., Cole, V., Colangelo, N., Assouline, S. G., & Russell, D. W. (1994). Perceived parental social support and academic achievement: An attachment theory perspective. *Journal of Personality and Social Psychology, 66*(2), 369. https://doi.org/10.1037/0022-3514.66.2.369

Deci, E. L., & Ryan, R. M. (1985). *Intrinsic motivation and self-determination in human behavior.* Plenum Press.

Deci, E. L., & Ryan, R. M. (2000). The "what" and "why" of goal pursuits: Human needs and the self-determination of behavior. *Psychological Inquiry, 11*, 227–268. https://doi.org/10.1207/S15327965PLI1104_01

Deci, E. L., & Ryan, R. M. (2014). Autonomy and need satisfaction in close relationships: Relationships motivation theory. In N. Weinstein (Ed.), *Human motivation and interpersonal relationships: Theory, research, and application* (pp. 53–76). Springer.

Dennis, J. M., Phinney, J. S., & Chuateco, L. I. (2005). The role of motivation, parental support, and peer support in the academic success of ethnic minority first-generation college students. *Journal of College Student Development, 46*(3), 223–236. https://doi.org/10.1353/csd.2005.0023

Division of Violence Prevention. (2019). *Preventing adverse childhood experiences (ACEs): Leveraging the best available evidence.* National Center for Injury Prevention and Control, Centers for Disease Control and Prevention.

Duncan, J. M., Lucier-Greer, M., Ferraro, A. J., & Reed-Fitzke, K. (2019). The role of social support in predicting depression and task overload among college students. *Journal of Human Sciences and Extension, 7*(1), 180–194.

Fass, M. E., & Tubman, J. G. (2002). The influence of parental and peer attachment on college students' academic achievement. *Psychology in the Schools, 39*(5), 561–573. https://doi.org/10.1002/pits.10050

Flaster, A. (2018). Kids, college, and capital: Parental financial support and college choice. *Research in Higher Education, 59*(8), 979–1020. https://doi.org/10.1007/s11162-018-9496-0

Flaster, A. (2020). Expectations and incentives: Parental financial support for college during the transition to young adulthood. *Journal of Student Financial Aid, 49*(3), 4.

Grolnick, W. S., Ryan, R. M., & Deci, E. L. (1991). The inner resources for school performance: Motivational mediators of children's perceptions of their parents. *Journal of Educational Psychology, 83*, 508–517.

Hamermesh, D. S., Frazis, H., & Stewart, J. (2005). Data watch: The American Time Use Survey. *Journal of Economic Perspectives, 19*(1), 221–232. https://doi.org/10.1257/0895330053148029

Hamilton, L. T. (2013). More is more or more is less? Parental financial investments during college. *American Sociological Review, 78*(1), 70–95. https://doi.org/10.1177/0003122412472680

Hamilton, L., Roksa, J., & Nielsen, K. (2018). Providing a "leg up": Parental involvement and opportunity hoarding in college. *Sociology of Education, 91*(2), 111–131. https://doi.org/10.1177/0038040718759557

Harper, C., Zhu, H., & Marquez Kiyama, J. (2020). Parents and families of first-generation college students experience their own college transition. *Journal of Higher Education, 91*(4), 540–564. https://doi.org/10.1080/00221546.2019.1647583

Hartig, N., & Steigerwald, F. (2007). Understanding family roles and ethics in working with first-generation college students and their families. *Family Journal, 15*(2), 159–162. https://doi.org/10.1177/1066480706297955

Hinojosa, R., Nguyen, J., Sellers, K., & Elassar, H. (2019). Barriers to college success among students that experienced adverse childhood events. *Journal of American College Health, 67*(6), 531–540. https://doi.org/10.1080/07448481.2018.1498851

Holt, L. J. (2014). Attitudes about help-seeking mediate the relation between parent attachment and academic adjustment in first-year college students. *Journal of College Student Development, 55*(4), 418–423. https://doi.org/10.1353/csd.2014.0039

Kahn, J., Kasky-Hernández, L., Ambrose, P., & French, S. (2017). Stress, depression, and anxiety among transitioning college students: The family as a protective factor. *Journal of the First-Year Experience & Students in Transition, 29*(2), 11–25.

Liem, J. H., Cavell, E. C., & Lustig, K. (2010). The influence of authoritative parenting during adolescence on depressive symptoms in young adulthood: Examining the mediating roles of self- development and peer support. *Journal of Genetic Psychology, 171*(1), 73–92. https://doi.org/10.1080/00221320903300379

Lindell, A. K., Campione-Barr, N., & Killoren, S. E. (2017). Implications of parent–child relationships for emerging adults' subjective feelings about adulthood. *Journal of Family Psychology, 31*, 810–820. https://doi.org/10.1037/fam0000328

Locke, J. Y., Campbell, M. A., & Kavanagh, D. (2012). Can a parent do too much for their child? An examination by parenting professionals of the concept of overparenting. *Journal of Psychologists and Counsellors in Schools, 22*(2), 249–265. https://doi-org/10.1017/jgc.2012.29

London, H. B. (1989). Breaking away: A study of first-generation college students and their families. *American Journal of Education, 97*(2), 144–170. https://doi.org/10.1086/443919

Love, K. (2008). Parental attachments and psychological distress among African American college students. *Journal of College Student Development, 49*(1), 31–40. https://doi.org/10.1353/csd.2008.0000

Lowe, K., & Arnett, J. J. (2020). Failure to grow up, failure to pay? Parents' views of conflict over money with their emerging adults. *Journal of Family Issues, 41*(3), 359–382. https://doi.org/10.1177/0192513X19876061

Lowe, K., Dotterer, A. M., & Francisco, J. (2015). "If I pay, I have a say!": Parental payment of college education and its association with helicopter parenting. *Emerging Adulthood, 3*, 286–290. https://doi.org/10.1177/2167696815579831

Luyckx, K., Soenens, B., Vansteenkiste, M., Goossens, L., & Berzonsky, M. D. (2007). Parental psychological control and dimensions of identity formation in emerging adulthood. *Journal of Family Psychology, 21*, 546–550. https://doi.org/10.1037/0893-3200.21.3.546

Mattanah, J. F., Hancock, G. R., & Brand, B. L. (2004). Parental attachment, separation-individuation, and college student adjustment: A structural equation analysis of mediational effects. *Journal of Counseling Psychology, 51*(2), 213. https://doi.org/10.1037/0022-0167.51.2.213

Mattanah, J. F., Lopez, F. G., & Govern, J. M. (2011). The contributions of parental attachment bonds to college student development and adjustment: A meta-analytic review. *Journal of Counseling Psychology, 58*(4), 565. https://doi.org/10.1037/a0024635

Melendez, M. C., & Melendez, N. B. (2010). The influence of parental attachment on the college adjustment of White, Black, and Latina/Hispanic women: A cross-cultural investigation. *Journal of College Student Development, 51*(4), 419–435. https://doi.org/10.1353/csd.0.0144

Mersky, J. P., Topitzes, J., & Reynolds, A. J. (2013). Impacts of adverse childhood experiences on health, mental health, and substance use in early adulthood: A cohort study of an urban, minority sample in the US. *Child Abuse & Neglect, 37*(11), 917–925. https://doi.org/10.1016/j.chiabu.2013.07.011

Mitchell, J., & Abraham, M. (2018). Parental mental illness and the transition to college: Coping, psychological adjustment, and parent–child relationships. *Journal of Child and Family Studies, 27*(9), 2966–2977. https://doi.org/10.1007/s10826-018-1133-1

Mounts, N. S., Valentiner, D. P., Anderson, K. L., & Boswell, M. K. (2006). Shyness, sociability, and parental support for the college transition: Relation to adolescents' adjustment. *Journal of Youth and Adolescence, 35*, 68–77. https://doi.org/10.1007/s10964-005-9002-9

Nelson, L. J., Padilla-Walker, L. M., & Nielson, M. G. (2015). Is hovering smothering or loving? An examination of parental warmth as a moderator of relations between helicopter parenting and emerging adults' indices of adjustment. *Emerging Adulthood, 3*, 282–285. https://doi.org/10.1177/2167696815576458

Nichols, L., & Islas, A. (2016). Pushing and pulling emerging adults through college: College generational status and the influence of parents and others in the first year. *Journal of Adolescent Research, 31*(1), 59–95. https://doi.org/10.1007/s10964-005-9002-9

Padilla-Walker, L. M., & Nelson, L. J. (2012). Black hawk down?: Establishing helicopter parenting as a distinct construct from other forms of parental control during emerging adulthood. *Journal of Adolescence, 35*, 1177–1190. https://doi.org/10.1016/j.adolescence.2012.03.007

Padilla-Walker, L. M., Nelson, L. J., & Carroll, J. S. (2012). Affording emerging adulthood: Parental financial assistance of their college-aged children. *Journal of Adult Development, 19*(1), 50–58. https://doi.org/10.1007/s10804-011-9134-y

Pedersen, D. (2017). Parental autonomy support and college student academic outcomes. *Journal of Child and Family Studies, 26*(9), 2589–2601. https://doi.org/10.1007/s10826-017-0750-4

Pinquart, M., & Kauser, R. (2018). Do the associations of parenting styles with behavior problems and academic achievement vary by culture? Results from a meta-analysis. *Cultural Diversity and Ethnic Minority Psychology, 24*, 75–100. https://doi.org/10.1037/cdp0000149

Pittman, L. D., & Richmond, A. (2008). University belonging, friendship quality, and psychological adjustment during the transition to college. *Journal of Experimental Education, 76*(4), 343–362. https://doi.org/10.3200/jexe.76.4.343-362

Pizzolato, J. E., & Hicklen, S. (2011). Parent involvement: Investigating the parent-child relationship in Millennial college students *Journal of College Student Development, 52*(6), 671–686. https://doi.org/10.1353/csd.2011.0081

Odenweller, K. G., Booth-Butterfield, M., & Weber, K. (2014). Investigating helicopter parenting, family environments, and relational outcomes for Millennials. *Communication Studies, 65*(4), 407–425. http://dx.doi.org/10.1080/10510974.2013.811434

Shoup, R., Gonyea, B., & Kuh, G. (2009). Helicopter parents: Examining the impact of highly involved parents on student engagement and educational outcomes. Paper presented at the 49th Annual Forum of the Association for Institutional Research Atlanta, Georgia June 1, 2009.

Thompson, K. V., & Verdino, J. (2019). An exploratory study of self-efficacy in community college students. *Community College Journal of Research and Practice, 43*(6), 476–479.

Reed, K. (2017). *Modern parent college involvement trends: A brief study on how different types of parents and their students communicate, to partner for success in college.* CampusESP. https://docsend.com/view/kwu4zw7

Reed, K., Duncan, J., Lucier-Greer, M., Fixelle, C., & Ferraro, A.J. (2016). Helicopter parenting and emerging adult self-efficacy: Implications for mental and physical health. *Journal of Child and Family Studies, 25*, 3136–3149. https://doi.org/10.1007/s10826-016-0466-x

Reed, K., Ferraro, A. J., Lucier-Greer, M., & Barber, C. (2015). Adverse family influences on emerging adult depressive symptoms: A stress process approach to identifying intervention points. *Journal of Child and Family Studies, 24*, 2710–2720. http://doi.org/10.1007/s10826-014-0073-7

Renzulli, L., & Barr, A. (2017). Adapting to family setbacks: Malleability of students' and parents' educational expectations. *Social Problems, 64*(3), 351–372. https://doi.org/10.1093/socpro/spw052

Rothbaum, F., Rosen, K., Ujiie, T., & Uchida, N. (2002). Family systems theory, attachment theory, and culture. *Family Process, 41*(3), 328–350. https://doi.org/10.1111/j.1545-5300.2002.41305.x

Ryan, R. M., & Deci, E. L. (2002). Overview of self-determination theory: An organismic dialectical perspective. In E. L. Deci & R. M. Ryan (Eds.), *Handbook of self-determination research* (pp. 3–33). University of Rochester Press.

Sarigiani, P., Trumbell, J., & Camarena, P. (2013). Electronic communications technologies and the transition to college: Links to parent-child attachment and adjustment. *Journal of the First-Year Experience & Students in Transition, 25*(1), 35–60.

Schiffrin, H. H., Liss, M., Miles-McLean, H., Geary, K. A., Erchull, M. J., & Tashner, T. (2014). Helping or hovering? The effects of helicopter parenting on college students' well-being. *Journal of Child and Family Studies, 23*, 548–557. https://doi.org/10.1007/s10826-013-9716-3

Segrin, C., Givertz, M., Swaitkowski, P., & Montgomery, N. (2015). Overparenting is associated with child problems and a critical family environment. *Journal of Child and Family Studies, 24*(2), 470–479. https://doi.org/10.1007/s10826-013-9858-3

Segrin, C., Woszidlo, A., Givertz, M., & Montgomery, N. (2013). Parent and child traits associated with overparenting. *Journal of Social and Clinical Psychology, 32*, 569–595. https://doi.org/10.1521/jscp.2013.32.6.569

Stein, C., Osborn, L., & Greenberg, S. (2016). Understanding young adults' reports of contact with their parents in a digital world: Psychological and familial relationship factors. *Journal of Child and Family Studies, 25*, 1802–1814. https://doi.org/10.1007/s10826-016-0366-0

Thomas, A. L., & Brausch, A. M. (2020). Family and peer support moderates the relationship between distress tolerance and suicide risk in black college students. *Journal of American College Health, 45*(4), 1–8. https://doi.org/10.1080/07448481.2020.1786096

Urry, S. A., Nelson, L. J., & Padilla-Walker, L. M. (2011). Mother knows best: Psychological control, child disclosure, and maternal knowledge in emerging adulthood. *Journal of Family Studies, 17*, 157–173. https://doi.org/10.5172/jfs.2011.17.2.157 U.S. Department of Education, Institute of Education Sciences, National Center for Education Statistics. (2016). *Digest of Education Statistics, 2015* (NCES Publication No. 2016-014). https://nces.ed.gov/programs/digest/d15/

van Ingen, D. J., Freiheit, S. R., Steinfeldt, J. A., Moore, L. L., Wimer, D. J., Knutt, A. D., Scapinello, S., & Roberts, A. (2015). Helicopter parenting: The effect of an overbearing caregiving style on peer attachment and self-efficacy. *Journal of College Counseling, 18*, 7–20. https://doi.org/10.1002/j.2161-1882.2015.00065.x

Workman, J. (2015). Parental influence on exploratory students' college choice, major, and career decision making. *College Student Journal, 49*(1), 23–30.

Yuan, S., Weiser, D., & Fischer, A. (2016). Self-efficacy, parent–child relationships, and academic performance: A comparison of European American and Asian American college students. *Social Psychology of Education, 19*(2), 261–280. https://doi.org/10.1007/s11218-015-9330-x

4

"I Took a Screenshot"

Experiences with Technology In and Out of the Classroom

Joan A. Swanson and Allison A. Buskirk-Cohen

To work effectively with emerging adults, higher education professionals need to understand the influence of technology on their development. The prevalence and dominance of technology in the lives of contemporary emerging adults is an unparalleled sociological change from previous generations in this age group. Many labels have been coined for this generation of digital users (Jones & Healing, 2010), such as millennials (Strauss & Howe, 1997), the net generation (Tapscott, 1998), the iGeneration (Twenge, 2014), and digital natives (Prensky, 2001). However, Bayne and Ross (2007) claim that change is inevitable from one generation to the next and these stereotypical titles are only connected to marketing aimed at educators. Regardless, these 18- to 29-year-old individuals are currently experiencing a world in which for them technology impacts nearly every aspect of their daily lives. For these emerging adults the internet has always been in existence and mobile devices were a part of their formative years (Mcmillan & Morrison, 2006). Swanson and Walker (2015) found technology to have a pervasive influence on emerging adult work, leisure, education, social interaction, and health. Much like their skin, for emerging adults, technology is necessary, always present, fulfilling essential roles, and yet not always recognized as such (Swanson, 2019). This chapter focuses on the technology experiences of today's emerging adults—both in and out of the higher education classroom. We will describe how technology impacts sense of self, relationships, mental health, and learning. Then we will present a case study to apply this knowledge and provide guiding questions.

During the 2010–2020 time period, technological advancements and varied uses of technology were marked by some of the following: the iPad was released (2010); new versions of iPhones and iOS were introduced almost yearly; technological wearables surfaced for a wide variety of on-the-move

Joan A. Swanson and Allison A. Buskirk-Cohen, *"I Took a Screenshot"* In: *Cultivating Student Success.* Edited by: Tisha A. Duncan and Allison A. Buskirk-Cohen, Oxford University Press. © Oxford University Press 2022. DOI: 10.1093/oso/9780197586693.003.0005 computing purposes (e.g., the Apple Watch in 2015); mobile gaming, as well as virtual and augmented reality, advanced with Oculus Quest (2020); and new frontiers in technology enhanced commerce activity (e.g., Google Pay and the mobile wallet were established in 2018; http://anddum.com/timeline/history_short.htm). The pervasiveness of these technological advancements potentially impacted the lives of emerging adults daily; thus, it is important to gain a deeper understanding of what has been studied about emerging adults in relationship to their technology use.

Technology Developments and Divide

With so many components of higher education moving online (e.g., orientation, coursework), it is critical to examine the assumption that all of today's emerging adults are part of a technologically savvy generation. Research on the idea of "digital natives" has revealed incredible diversity and insights into students' experience of technology in and out of the classroom (Bennett & Maton, 2010). Indeed, advanced interaction with the internet is not predicted by generation alone (Brown & Czerniewicz, 2010; Helsper & Eynon, 2010). In fact, we know that emerging adults vary widely in their experiences with technology. Research on the digital divide centers around issues of access, use, and outcomes (Robinson et al., 2020). Even in places where access is widespread, inequalities still exist in terms of network quality and device access. Furthermore, there is differentiated usage and skill divides.

Students may not be as skilled with technology as is often assumed (e.g., Kennedy et al., 2009). Swanson and Walker (2015) explored the distinction between academic and nonacademic patterns of technology use and found frequent difficulty transferring skills from one type of technology use to other uses. Everyday technology-based activities, such as posting photographs and videos on Instagram, may not prepare students well for academic practices, such as critically analyzing sources for a research report, for example. Additionally, Swanson and colleagues (2017) recommend avoiding generalized assumptions about digital technology competency since preferences and patterns of technology use will vary from person to person. Online tutorials on financial aid, campus policies, adding/dropping courses, and other aspects of college life may not be accessible or understandable to all emerging adults, and higher education professionals must be prepared to address the variation in their needs.

Impact on Self

As noted in earlier chapters, the exploration and development of identity is a key feature in emerging adult development (Arnett, 2004). The access to social media gives youth and emerging adults an opportunity to express themselves and to have immediate feedback. Using technology, especially social media, sets the stage for social comparison, thus impacting self-concepts and ultimately self-esteem. According to the Pew Research Center (2019), emerging adults are the highest users of social media sites, following trends from earlier years (e.g., Duggan & Smith, 2014). Among individuals ages 18 to 24, 90% report using YouTube (Perrin & Anderson, 2019). The next most common online platform for this age group is Facebook (76%), followed closely by Instagram (75%) and Snapchat (73%). Shane-Simpson et al. (2018) examined the types of sites used and why college students prefer certain social media sites. Their results highlighted the popularity of Instagram for college students and, more specifically, for women. For higher education professionals considering how to reach students through social media, this research demonstrates that gender, age, affordances on specific sites, and privacy concerns all predict social media preferences.

Social networks were historically differentiated largely by residential proximity. With the onset of increased social media, these networks can go beyond the physical residential proximity. Thus, emerging adults can forge relationships with others who may not be in their geographic proximity, which could potentially result in an expansion of their social capital. Social capital is viewed as "connections among individuals—social networks and the norms of reciprocity and trustworthiness that arise from them" (Putnam, 2000, p. 19). Manago and Melton (2020) analyzed how college students in the United States viewed topics of mass personal self-disclosure on a social network site (i.e., Facebook). Their analyses showed how valuing self-expression greatly informed participants' decision-making about self-disclosure and was important for their development of bridging social capital.

Social media sites also may offer advantages to specific marginalized groups of emerging adults. Students with marginalized identities report greater distress, particularly in the recent extremist sociopolitical environment (Albright & Hurd, 2020). These students may find solace and a sense of community through social media. In 2014, for example, an online student activist movement, "I, Too, Am," revealed everyday racism experienced by Black college students. It began with Harvard University's Kuumba Singer's multimedia campaign to open dialogue about racial inclusion and spread to other institutions of higher education throughout the United States. As another example, Bates et al. (2020) interviewed LGBTQ+ undergraduates on their social media usage and identity development. Their interviews highlighted how social media provides LGBTQ+ youth with regular access to safe environments. Social media also provided an opportunity to seek identities for LGBTQ+ youth that matched their pre-existing sense of self in this study.

It may be helpful to view this research in light of social identity theory, proposed by Tajfel and Turner in the late 1970s (Tajfel, 1978; Tajfel & Turner, 1979). It suggests that individuals internalize a group membership so that it becomes part of their self-concept. Researchers have suggested that individuals who occupy less privileged positions in their cultural communities, such as women, BIPOC (Black, Indigenous, and People of Color), and LGBTQ+, are more aware of their social identities than others (e.g., Azmitia et al., 2008). While certainly there are many important influences on identity formation, it may be significant to consider the role of social media, particularly for emerging adults with marginalized identities. For students struggling with their identity, social media may offer new experiences and opportunities for support.

Impact on Relationships

Often identity development in emerging adulthood is directly linked to areas of love, work, and worldviews (Arnett, 2015). Increasingly, each of these areas is intertwined with the emerging adult's technology use, shaping how emerging adults relate to others. Technology-driven communication fuels relational connections, conversations, and opportunities, and within this virtual context emerging adults can explore and experiment. Researchers have noted that social media responds to a basic human need to belong (Baumeister & Leary, 1995) and that students' need to belong has been associated with their use of social media and smartphones (Kim et al., 2016). This section will focus on how technology influences the maintenance and dissolution of interpersonal relationships for emerging adults.

Early research on texting of college students showed that the majority sent messages related to maintaining friendships, romances, and other social relationships (Thurlow, 2003). One study found that college students reported that text messaging is their most preferred method of contact with friends (Harrison & Gilmore, 2012). They also viewed it as a mode of communication with family, friends, romantic partners, and other significant individuals (Harrison & Gilmore, 2012). They seem to prefer using cell phones for interacting with close friends (Brown et al., 2016).

However, more recent research suggests that cell phone use may have a negative impact on relationships. Pryzybylski and Weinstein (2013) found that college students who were meeting for the first time reported lower feelings of trust and empathic understanding when there was a cell phone in the room. Frequency of texting an individual is negatively associated with feelings of relationship satisfaction among college students (Angstermichael & Lester, 2010). Also, for friends who text each other while physically being in the same room, Brown et al. (2016) found that more phone use was associated with lower-quality friendship interactions. Among romantic partners, more than half (52%) of 18- to 29-year-olds report that their partner is at least sometimes distracted by their phone when they are trying to engage in conversation (Vogels & Anderson, 2020). Researchers across studies speculate that phones prevent students from fully engaging with their partner.

Technology also has led to different ways of dissolving a relationship—specifically, the technique of ghosting. Ghosting involves vanishing from a relationship without notice by avoiding technologically mediated contact with a partner instead of expressing the desire to end the relationship (Koessler, 2018; LeFebvre et al., 2019). This phenomenon is not surprising considering that emerging adults appear to have less structured and scripted relationship development (Stanley et al., 2011). LeFebre and colleagues (2019) asked emerging adults about their experiences with ghosting. The majority of participants reported being both an initiator and noninitiator. It is a form of social rejection that can be emotionally distressing and can harm both partners. Ghosting breakups have been characterized by greater use of avoidance/withdrawal and distant/mediated communication tactics (Koessler, 2018). Emerging adults describe a tension between intimacy and isolation (Arnett, 2004; Beyers & Seiffge-Krenke, 2010) where they have a connection to positive relationship formation (such as closeness and connectedness) but also to negative experiences (such as fear of intimacy and commitment; LeFebvre & Carmack, 2020).

All in all, researchers question the implications these behaviors have for relationship readiness and commitment. How do these behaviors translate to the way students interact with different facets of campus life? Students who struggle to communicate appropriately with faculty and staff may be having trouble shifting from one context to another. The cell phone behaviors that are considered appropriate with friends, for example, have very different meanings in the context of a student-faculty interaction. Faculty who wonder why students struggling with a class suddenly stop attending might view the situation in terms of relationship dissolution, or ghosting. Perhaps students' hesitancy to commit to a major (or an institution) might be better understood in terms of relationship readiness and commitment. A more nuanced understanding of how technology has influenced relationships among emerging adults may help higher education professionals work more effectively with them.

Impact on Mental Health

Many campuses struggle with providing adequate mental health resources for their students, whose needs seem to continue to increase every year. Much of the recent research on emerging adult mental health has documented relationships between technology, internalizing problems (e.g., anxiety and depression), and externalizing problems (e.g., alcohol and drug use; e.g., Abi-Jaoude et al., 2020; Keles et al., 2020). For example, in a large study of emerging adults in the United States, Vannucci et al. (2017) examined the impact of social media usage on anxiety symptoms and severity. They found that more time spent using social media was associated with greater symptoms of anxiety. Their results also indicated that more daily social media use was associated with a greater likelihood of participants scoring above the anxiety-severity clinical cut-off. In another large study, Vannucci et al., (2019) found that individuals who used a higher number of different social media platforms reported more anxiety symptoms, depressive symptoms, total alcohol consumption, and drug use. Interestingly, Facebook use was associated uniquely with depressive symptoms, while Snapchat use was associated with substance use. Taken together, these findings highlight the complexity of understanding how social media impacts mental health.

One possible mechanism for the link between technology use and poor mental health may be the increased risk for online harassment and bullying. Rates of online victimization among college students vary widely, ranging from about 4% to 92% depending on operationalization and sampling (e.g., Bennett et al., 2011). In one study of cyberbullying among college students, 8.6% reported being victims of cyberbullying and they scored higher than matched controls on depression, anxiety, and other negative mental health indices (Schenk & Fremouw, 2012). In one study of undergraduates' experiences and responses to online harassment, researchers found that online harassment is linked to issues of intimate partner violence (Lindsay et al., 2016). They also found that female students who were harassed by a partner associated that online harassment with experiences of fear and with increased feelings of anxiety and depression. Males in their study also experienced feelings of anxiety and depression but did not associate them with fear. Additional research is needed to understand the role of gender, technology use, online harassment, and poor mental health outcomes.

One potential silver lining to this section is the possibility of using technology to promote positive health outcomes. Salzano and colleagues (2021) found that the quarantine experience due to the COVID-19 pandemic had many psychological drawbacks due to isolation; however, many young people successfully combated those feelings when they turned to technology and specifically social media to stay connected to the rest of the world. Elmer and colleagues (2020) found the type of mental health issues during the pandemic shifted from social anxiety related to the fear of missing out to worries about the health and safety of themselves and their loved ones. Social media became a channel to connect while being socially distant. Additionally, in the recent pandemic, researchers have noted the potential to promote positive mental health has increased as young people turn to social media for health-related information (Goodyear et al., 2018; Lattie et al., 2019; O'Reilly et al., 2019). Wearables and mobile apps are increasingly useful in health tracking and in treating many health concerns, including mental health. Since most young adults have access to mobile devices, digital health interventions could be quite useful in community mental health services (Aschbrenner et al., 2019). These are especially useful in identifying signs of mental health deterioration and facilitating intervention (Dewa et al., 2019). Higher educational professionals can utilize technology to promote positive health behaviors while also recognizing the potential problems that may occur and educating students about them.

Impact on Learning

During the past two decades, technology has become an integrated part of most colleges' and universities' learning environment. For example, most teaching in higher education is supported by learning management systems (LMS), such as Google Workspace, Canvas, Blackboard, and Moodle, which provide virtual bulletin boards, document storehouses, collaboration tools, and opportunities for assessment (Schroeder et al., 2010). Many educators also use social software applications in their courses, such as blogs, wikis, and social bookmarking tools.

Studies have found positive aspects to integrating information technology in the classroom. For example, asynchronous instructional technology provides learners with additional time to think critically and reflectively (Robinson & Hullinger, 2008). A number of studies find associations between technology use and engagement for learners. Chen et al. (2010) reported positive relationships between the use of learning technology, student engagement, and learning outcomes. Also, when comparing first-year students to seniors, their results suggest that the use of technology has a stronger impact earlier in the college experience. Junco et al. (2011) also found that technology can facilitate student engagement. Specifically, they found that using Twitter for various types of academic and cocurricular discussion facilitated greater engagement and higher semester grade point averages.

However, research also shows that electronic media exposure, such as video game use and engagement with social networking sites, may not be helpful and can even be detrimental to academic achievement (Uzun & Kilis, 2019). Jacobsen and Forste (2011) found a negative relationship between the use of various electronic media and first-semester grades. The majority of students report using electronic media to multitask, which actually serves as a detractor. Specially, a majority of the students reported using electronic media while in class, studying, or doing homework. The key in understanding the impact of technology or media use may be connected to the level of engagement. For example, Dunn and Kennedy's work (2019) suggests that it is not simply usage that matters; instead, it is engagement with technology-enhanced learning that predicts grades. However, some researchers suggest the investment in technology-based classrooms may not be financially worthwhile. For example, Nicol et al. (2018) found no difference in student grades when comparing a high-technology-based active learning classroom environment and a low-technology-based active learning classroom. It was not the amount of technological tools utilized such as computers, clickers, and projectors that mattered; it was the actual engagement in learning activities with or without those items.

Yet, there may be times when technology offers unique educational opportunities, such as with the COVID-19 pandemic. Colleges and universities experienced disruption to and closure of their courses and activities beginning in the spring of 2020 (Harper, 2020; Sahu, 2020), and the opening of institutions in the fall 2020 semester brought new challenges and risks for transmission on campuses while continuing to educate students and provide other services. Many institutions transitioned various courses and programs to face-to-face, synchronous online delivery (Ali, 2020; Sahu, 2020). For many, this was a new frontier in educational instruction. The shift to online teaching raised questions for faculty about their ability to cope effectively with technology, and for institutions about their infrastructure and resources to facilitate online teaching and learning (Cutri & Mena, 2020; O'Keefe et al., 2020). Also, there are questions about how to conduct valid and reliable assessment, specifically for courses originally designed for in-person, face-to-face-learning (Sahu, 2020).

Research on how students are responding to these changes is mixed. Early research on students' perceptions indicates that students feel that their professors adapted and communicated changes in course content effectively during the online transition (Murphy et al., 2020). However, after the initial transition, many students had overall negative attitudes toward online learning and preferred face-to-face learning (Patricia, 2020). Many emerging adult students have expressed negative emotional reactions to remote teaching and learning, including uncertainty, anxiety, and nervousness (Murphy et al., 2020). Furthermore, there continue to be problems with access. Many institutions have provided students with laptops, tablets, and other technological devices (McMurtrie, 2020), but many lower-income students lack access to Wi-Fi and reliable high-speed internet (Flaherty, 2020).

Conclusion

Many emerging adults are at a place where technology use is ubiquitous, touching every corner of their lives. Technology use has become central in daily functioning, and for many, technology feels like an extension of themselves. Emerging adult technology use impacts their social emotional development by influencing conceptions of themselves and others, as well as serving as a widely used medium for comparison and communication. Additionally, technology use is intricately connected to learning through both preference and necessity. The mental health of emerging adults is not only impacted through their technology use but also evidenced in their relationships and projected futures. The ramification of ubiquitous technology use and the growing dependence upon technology among emerging adults necessitate continued attention and analysis.

The following section contains a case study that illustrates many of the common issues faced by emerging adults. This case study provides insight into the experiences and decisions that are commonly wrestled with among many emerging adults. As you review the case study, consider the impact of different modes and patterns of technology use as well as the inequity within technological services and tools.

Case Study

Alex received a highly competitive scholarship to a private institution, where he is currently a first-year student. Alex has been residing on campus, though he has not made many friends in the dorm. Alex tends to keep to himself, partially because he assumes he has little in common with the other students. Knowing the high cost of the school's tuition, Alex assumes the majority of students are from wealthy families. They tend to wear trendy clothes and drive expensive cars, neither of which Alex possesses. He also has trouble making friends because he does not participate in sports or other activities. The majority of his time is dedicated to his studies so that he can maintain his scholarship. However, in this fall semester, Alex has encountered many problems with technology and does not know how to handle these problems.

To begin, Alex has been using an old laptop since high school, but it recently broke. The cost of repairing it is almost the same as purchasing a new one—but Alex does not have the money for either option. He cannot ask his parents for assistance; his father recently lost his job and his mother earns minimum wage. His family simply does not have extra funds to spare. Additionally, his parents have started questioning whether a college degree is worthwhile, from a financial perspective. They are very proud of Alex's accomplishments but wonder if it would be best for him to delay his college plans. They have suggested he should possibly come home to work at a local job and help contribute to the family. Alex truly loves learning and is dedicated toward his degree, but his family's questions have planted doubts in his mind.

From a practical perspective, Alex now uses his cell phone to complete all of his coursework. Due to the COVID-19 pandemic, several of his classes have switched entirely to remote learning. Additionally, the school's library has very limited hours, so Alex cannot rely on their computers for use. Instead, he often goes to public parking lots to access Wi-Fi so that he can livestream his classes. In the majority of his classes, Alex continues to perform well. However, one class requires a specific type of software that cannot be downloaded to a mobile phone. Alex is contemplating dropping this class, but that will impact his overall grade point average and potentially place his scholarship at risk.

Alex is extremely worried about what to do and does not have many people he can turn to for support. He had started talking with a girl on campus named Kristine, but she no longer responds to Alex's texts and has blocked Alex on social media. They had met through Instagram—Alex loves photography and posted images of campus on his account. Kristine had liked his posts and began following him. Then, she started commenting on images and they exchanged messages. They met for coffee and became inseparable. Alex confided in her about his worries, and she was great at listening and encouraging him. He appreciated the intimacy—both emotional and physical. Suddenly, she just disappeared and Alex realized he had been ghosted. He feels more alone than he did before.

With all of the issues weighing heavily upon Alex, he is now experiencing feelings of despair. He does not know what to do about the technology issues that stand in the way of his academic success. He has tried to problem-solve with the resources he has, but these struggles are now reflected in the quality of his academic work. He feels the weight of having financial needs as well as discord and pressure from his family. Alex feels alone, rejected, and misunderstood. This past weekend Alex turned to alcohol to help drown out these feelings. While drunk, he posted inappropriate messages about and photos of Kristine to a few social media sites connected with the institution.

The next morning, Alex realized his error and removed his postings, but someone had taken screenshots and reported them as violations of the student conduct code. Alex is now facing a review board and has shared all of this background information. He feels ashamed of his recent behavior and is also struggling with why his relationship with Kristine failed and how to handle his financial challenges. He is questioning if he should have ever begun this academic path or stayed closer to home working jobs as he could find them. Alex is unsure where to turn or what to do next.

Guiding Questions

1. After reviewing the case study, in what ways do you see technology used as an asset?
2. In what ways is technology use causing Alex to struggle?
3. What are your institution's policies regarding social media use? Are they in line with the ways in which emerging adults use technology today?
4. What technological resources are needed for students to be successful at your institution? Are they accessible?
5. How does your institution support students who may face issues of equity with technology?
6. What are the advantages and disadvantages to incorporating technology use in academic settings?

References

Abi-Jaoude, E., Naylor, K. T., & Pignatiello, A. (2020). Smartphones, social media use and youth mental health. *CMAJ: Canadian Medical Association Journal [Journal de l'Association Medicale Canadienne]*, *192*(6), E136–E141.

Albright, J. N., & Hurd, N. M. (2020). Marginalized identities, Trump-related distress, and the mental health of underrepresented college students. *American Journal of Community Psychology*, *65*(3–4), 381–396.

Ali, W. (2020). Online and remote learning in higher education institutes: A necessity in light of COVID-19 pandemic. *Higher Education*, *10*(3), 16–25.

Angstermichael, A., & Lester, F. (2010). An exploratory study of students' use of cell phones, texting, and social networking sites. *Psychological Reports, 107*, 402–404.

Arnett, J. J. (2004). *Emerging adulthood: The winding road from late teens through the twenties.* Oxford University Press.

Arnett, J. J. (2015). College students as emerging adults: The developmental implications of the college context. *Emerging Adulthood*, *4*(3), 219–222.

Aschbrenner, K. A., Naslund, J. A., Tomlinson, E. F., Kinney, A., Pratt, S. I., & Brunette, M. F. (2019). Adolescents' use of digital technologies and preferences for mobile health coaching in public mental health settings. *Frontiers in Public Health*, *7*, 178. https://doi.org/10.3389/fpubh.2019.00178

Azmitia, M., Syed, M., & Radmacher, K. (2008). On the intersection of personal and social identities: Introduction and evidence from a longitudinal study of emerging adults. In M. Azmitia, M. Syed, & K. Radmacher (Eds.), *The intersections of personal and social identities: New Directions for Child and Adolescent Development* (No. 120, pp. 1–16).

Bates, A., Hobman, T., & Bell, B. T. (2020). "Let me do what I please with it . . . Don't decide my identity for me": LGBTQ+ youth experiences of social media in narrative identity development. *Journal of Adolescent Research*, *35*(1), 51–83.

Baumeister, R. F., & Leary, M. R. (1995). The need to belong: Desire for interpersonal attachments as a fundamental human motivation. *Psychological Bulletin*, *117*(3), 497.

Bayne, S. & Ross, J. (2007). The 'digital native' and 'digital immigrant': A dangerous opposition. Paper presented at the Annual Conference of the Society for Research into Higher Education, Liverpool, UK, 9–11 December, 2007. Retrieved from: http://www.malts.ed.ac.uk/staff/sian/natives_final.pdf

Bennett, D. C., Guran, E. L., Ramos, M. C., & Margolin, G. (2011). College students' electronic victimization in friendships and dating relationships: Anticipated distress and associations with risky behaviors. *Violence and Victims*, *26*(4), 410–429.

Bennett, S., & Maton, K. (2010). Beyond the "digital natives" debate: Towards a more nuanced understanding of students' technology experiences. *Journal of Computer Assisted Learning*, *26*(5), 321–331.

Beyers, W., & Seiffge-Krenke, I. (2010). Does identity precede intimacy? Testing Erikson's theory on romantic development in emerging adults of the 21st century. *Journal of Adolescent Research, 25*, 387–415. doi:10.1177/0743558410361370

Brown, C., & Czerniewicz, L. (2010). Debunking the "digital native": Beyond digital apartheid, towards digital democracy. *Journal of Computer Assisted Learning*, *26*(5), 357–369.

Brown, G., Manago, A. M., & Trimble, J. E. (2016). Tempted to text: College students' mobile phone use during a face-to-face interaction with a close friend. *Emerging Adulthood*, *4*(6), 440–443.

Chen, P. S. D., Lambert, A. D., & Guidry, K. R. (2010). Engaging online learners: The impact of Web-based learning technology on college student engagement. *Computers & Education*, *54*(4), 1222–1232.

Cutri, R. M., & Mena, J. (2020). A critical reconceptualization of faculty readiness for online teaching. *Distance Education, 41*(3), 361–380.

Dewa, L. H., Lavelle, M., Pickles, K., Kalorkoti, C., Jaques, J., Pappa, S., & Aylin, P. (2019). Young adults' perceptions of using wearables, social media and other technologies to detect worsening mental health: A qualitative study. *PLoS ONE, 14*(9), 1–14.

Duggan, M., & Smith, A. (2014). Cell Internet use 2013. Pew Research Center. http://pewinternet.org/Reports/2013/Cell-Internet.aspx

Dunn, T. J., & Kennedy, J. (2019). Technology enhanced learning in higher education: Motivations, engagement and academic achievement. *Computers & Education, 137*, 104–113. doi:10.1016/j.compedu.2019.04.004

Elmer, T., Mepham, K., & Stadtfeld, C. (2020). Students under lockdown: Comparisons of students' social networks and mental health before and during the COVID-19 crisis in Switzerland. *PLoS ONE, 15*(7), 1–22. doi.org/10.1371/journal.pone.0236337

Flaherty, C. (2020, May 8). Reserved: Internet parking, using Wi-Fri ready college parking lots is now a way of life for students with limited or no internet access. *Inside Higher Ed.* https://www.insidehighered.com/news/2020/05/08/parking-lot-wi-fi-way-life-many-students

Goodyear, V. A., Armour, K. M., & Wood, H. (2018). Young people and their engagement with health-related social media: New perspectives. *Sport, Education and Society, 24*(7), 673–688. doi:10.1080/13573322.2017.1423464.

Harper, S. R. (2020). COVID-19 and the racial equity implications of reopening college and university campuses. *American Journal of Education, 127*(1), 153–162.

Harrison, M. A., & Gilmore, A. L. (2012). U txt WHEN? College students' social contexts of text messaging. *Social Science Journal, 49*(4), 513–518. doi:10.1016/j.soscij.2012.05.003

Helsper, E. J., & Eynon, R. (2010). Digital natives: Where is the evidence? *British Educational Research Journal, 36*(3), 503–520.

Jacobsen, W. C., & Forste, R. (2011). The wired generation: Academic and social outcomes of electronic media use among university students. *Cyberpsychology, Behavior, and Social Networking, 14*, 275–280.

Jones, C., & Healing, G. (2010). Net generation students: agency and choice and the new technologies. *Journal of Computer Assisted Learning, 26*(5), 344–356.

Junco, R. R., Heiberger, G. G., & Loken, E. E. (2011). The effect of Twitter on college student engagement and grades. *Journal of Computer Assisted Learning, 27*, 119–132.

Keles, B., McCrae, N., & Grealish, A. (2020). A systematic review: The influence of social media on depression, anxiety and psychological distress in adolescents. *International Journal of Adolescence and Youth, 25*(1), 79–93.

Kennedy, G., Dalgarno, B., Bennett, S., Gray, K., Waycott, J., Judd, T., Bishop, A., Maton, K., Krause, K-L., & Chang, R. (2009). *Educating the net generation: A handbook of findings for practice and policy.* University of Melbourne Press.

Kim, Y., Wang, Y., & Oh, J. (2016). Digital media use and social engagement: How social media and smartphone use influence social activities of college students. *Cyberpsychology, Behavior, and Social Networking, 19*(4), 264–269. doi:10.1089/cyber.2015.0408

Koessler, R. B. (2018). *When your boo becomes a ghost: The association between breakup strategy and breakup role in experiences of relationship dissolution* [Master's thesis]. https://ir.lib.uwo.ca/cgi/viewcontent.cgi?article=7493&context=etd

Lattie, E. G., Lipson, S. K., & Eisenberg, D. (2019). Technology and college student mental health: Challenges and opportunities. *Frontiers in Psychiatry, 10*, 246.

LeFebvre, L. E., Allen, M., Rasner, R. D., Garstad, S., Wilms, A., & Parrish, C. (2019). Ghosting in emerging adults' romantic relationships: The digital dissolution disappearance strategy. *Imagination, Cognition and Personality, 39*(2), 125–150.

LeFebvre, L. E., & Carmack, H. J. (2020). Catching feelings: Exploring commitment (un) readiness in emerging adulthood. *Journal of Social and Personal Relationships, 37*(1), 143–162.

Lindsay, M., Booth, J. M., Messing, J. T., & Thaller, J. (2016). Experiences of online harassment among emerging adults: Emotional reactions and the mediating role of fear. *Journal of Interpersonal Violence, 31*(19), 3174–3195.

Manago, A. M., & Melton, C. J. (2020). Emerging adults' views on mass personal self-disclosure and their bridging social capital on Facebook. *Journal of Adolescent Research, 35*(1), 111–146.

McMillan, S. J., & Morrison, M. (2006). Coming of age with the internet: A qualitative exploration of how the internet has become an integral part of young people's lives. *New Media & Society, 8*(1), 73–95.

McMurtrie, B. (2020, April 6). Students without laptops, instructors without internet: How struggling colleges move online during COVID-19. *Chronicle of Higher Education*. https://www.chronicle.com/article/students-without-laptops-instructors-without-internet-how-struggling-colleges-move-online-during-covid-19/

Murphy, L., Eduljee, N. B., & Croteau, K. (2020). College student transition to synchronous virtual classes during the COVID-19 pandemic in Northeastern United States. *Pedagogical Research, 5*(4), 1–10.

Nicol, A. A., Owens, S. M., Le Coze, S. S., MacIntyre, A., & Eastwood, C. (2018). Comparison of high-technology active learning and low-technology active learning classrooms. *Active Learning in Higher Education, 19*(3), 253–265.

O'Keefe, L., Rafferty, J., Gunder, A., & Vignare, K. (2020). Delivering high-quality instruction online in response to COVID-19: Faculty playbook. *Online Learning Consortium*. https://files.eric.ed.gov/fulltext/ED605351.pdf

O'Reilly, M., Dogra, N., Hughes, J., Reilly, P., George, R., & Whiteman, N. (2019). Potential of social media in promoting mental health in adolescents. *Health Promotion International, 34*(5), 981–991.

Patricia, A. (2020). College students' use and acceptance of emergency online learning due to Covid-19. *International Journal of Educational Research Open*, 100011.

Perrin, A., & Anderson, M. (2019). Share of US adults using social media, including Facebook, is mostly unchanged since 2018. Pew Research Center. https://www.pewresearch.org/fact-tank/2019/04/10/share-of-u-s-adults-using-social-media-including-facebook-is-mostly-unchanged-since-2018/

Pew Research Center. (2019). Social media fact sheet. https://www.pewresearch.org/internet/fact-sheet/social-media/

Prensky, M. (2001). Digital natives, digital immigrants part 2: Do they really think differently?. *On the horizon.*

Przybylski, A. K., & Weinstein, N. (2013). Can you connect with me now? How the presence of mobile communication technology influences face-to-face conversation quality. *Journal of Social and Personal Relationships, 30*(3), 237–246.

Putnam, R. D. (2000). Bowling alone: America's declining social capital. In *Culture and politics* (pp. 223–234). Palgrave Macmillan.

Robinson, C. C., & Hullinger, H. (2008). New benchmarks in higher education: Student engagement in online learning. *Journal of Education for Business, 84*(2), 101–108.

Robinson, L., Schulz, J., Blank, G., Ragnedda, M., Ono, H., Hogan, B., . . . Yan, P. (2020). Digital inequalities 2.0: Legacy inequalities in the information age. *First Monday, 25*(7). doi.org/10.5210/fm.v25i7.10842

Sahu, P. (2020). Closure of universities due to coronavirus disease 2019 (COVID-19): Impact on education and mental health of students and academic staff. *Cureus, 12*(4), e7541. doi.org/10.7759/cureus.7541

Salzano, G., Passanisi, S., Pira, F., Sorrenti, L., La Monica, G., Pajno, G. B., Pecoraro, M., & Lombardo, F. (2021). Quarantine due to the COVID-19 pandemic from the perspective of adolescents: The crucial role of technology. *Italian Journal of Pediatrics, 47*(1), 1–5. doi.org/10.1186/s13052-021-00997-7

Schenk, A. M., & Fremouw, W. J. (2012). Prevalence, psychological impact, and coping of cyberbully victims among college students. *Journal of School Violence, 11*(1), 21–37.

Schroeder, A., Minocha, S., & Schneider, C. (2010). The strengths, weaknesses, opportunities and threats of using social software in higher and further education teaching and learning. *Journal of Computer Assisted Learning, 26*(3), 159–174.

Shane-Simpson, C., Manago, A., Gaggi, N., & Gillespie-Lynch, K. (2018). Why do college students prefer Facebook, Twitter, or Instagram? Site affordances, tensions between privacy and self-expression, and implications for social capital. *Computers in Human Behavior, 86,* 276–288.

Stanley, S. M., Rhoades, G. K., & Fincham, F. D. (2011). Understanding romantic relationship among emerging adults: The significant roles of cohabitation and ambiguity. In F. D. Fincham & M. Cui (Eds.), *Romantic relationships in emerging adulthood* (pp. 234–251). Cambridge University Press.

Strauss, W., & Howe, N. (1997). *The fourth turning: An American prophecy.* Broadway Books.

Swanson, J. A. (2019). Technology as skin. In M. F. Wright (Ed.), *Digital technology: Advance in research and applications.* Nova Publishing.

Swanson, J. A., Renes, S. L., & Strange, A. T. (2017). *I might not be as tech as you think: Digital versus print preferences.* Paper presented at the 14th International Conference on Cognition and Exploratory Learning in the Digital Age (CELDA), Vilamoura, Algarve, Portugal.

Swanson, J. A., & Walker, E. (2015). Academic versus non-academic emerging adult college student technology use. *Technology, Knowledge and Learning, 20*(2), 147–158. doi.org/10.1007/s10758-015-9258-4

Tajfel, H. E. (1978). *Differentiation between social groups: Studies in the social psychology of intergroup relations.* Academic Press.

Tajfel, H., & Turner, J. C. (1979). An integrative theory of intergroup conflict. In W. G. Austin & S. Worchel (Eds.), *The social psychology of intergroup relations* (pp. 33–47). Brooks Cole.

Tapscott, D. (1998). *Growing up digital: The rise of the net generation.* McGraw-Hill.

Thurlow, C. (2003). Generation Txt? The sociolinguistics of young people's text messaging. *Discourse Analysis Online, 1*(1), 30.

Twenge, J. (2014). *Generation me-revised and updated: Why today's young Americans are more confident, assertive, entitled—and more miserable than ever before.* Simon and Schuster.

Uzun, A. M., & Kilis, S. (2019). Does persistent involvement in media and technology lead to lower academic performance? Evaluating media and technology use in relation to multitasking, self-regulation and academic performance. *Computers in Human Behavior, 90,* 196–203.

Vannucci, A., Flannery, K. M., & Ohannessian, C. M. (2017). Social media use and anxiety in emerging adults. *Journal of Affective Disorders, 207,* 163–166.

Vannucci, A., Ohannessian, C. M., & Gagnon, S. (2019). Use of multiple social media platforms in relation to psychological functioning in emerging adults. *Emerging Adulthood, 7*(6), 501–506.

Vogels, E., & Anderson, M. (2020). Dating and relationships in the digital age. Pew Research Center. https://www.pewresearch.org/internet/2020/05/08/dating-and-relationships-in-the-digital-age/

5

"^^ KWIM? BRB"

How Do Emerging Adults Communicate Differently than Previous Generations?

Heather T. Rowan-Kenyon, Adam M. McCready,
Ana M. Martínez Alemán, and Allison Yarri

Contemporary college students constitute a generation of learners whose communication and academic and social lives are composed and performed through online communication (Rowan-Kenyon et al., 2016). Online spaces provide new generations of college-going students with the ability to create campus culture, form new relationships and deepen existing relationships, and extend their informational reach considerably (Martínez Alemán & Wartman, 2009). Technology and social media are woven into the everyday lives of college students. For emerging adults aged 18 to 24, Facebook, Snapchat, and Instagram are most popular with roughly 70% use across all three platforms, with reports that college students are using these apps multiple times per day. While these apps are the most widely used, there are many other apps popular with emerging adults that they use to communicate (Perrin & Anderson, 2019).

During the COVID-19 pandemic, emerging adults adapted the way they use technology and social media to communicate with and stay connected to friends, family, and their community. The majority of emerging adults said that the internet and phones were useful for staying connected but were not a replacement for in-person contact (Anderson & Vogels, 2020). In 2020, the internet and social media played a significant role in spreading information about the coronavirus, with 82% of emerging adults using the internet to search for information about the coronavirus and 44% of emerging adults using social media to share or repost information about the coronavirus (Anderson & Vogels, 2020).

Emerging adults' use of online sources to learn about COVID-19 is consistent with research related to current modalities of news consumption, as 76% of adults (18 to 49) who read the news prefer online sources to newspapers

Heather T. Rowan-Kenyon, Adam M. McCready, Ana M. Martínez Alemán, and Allison Yarri, *"^^ KWIM? BRB"* In: *Cultivating Student Success.* Edited by: Tisha A. Duncan and Allison A. Buskirk-Cohen, Oxford University Press. © Oxford University Press 2022. DOI: 10.1093/oso/9780197586693.003.0006

(Mitchell, 2018). More than two-thirds of Americans say that they get news on social media at least occasionally, though over half of Americans expect that news to be inaccurate (Shearer & Matsa, 2018). Across platforms, emerging adults (ages 18 to 29) make up the majority of Snapchat's news consumers, followed by 54% of Reddit's, 40% of Instagram's, 32% of Twitter's, 30% of Facebook's, and 23% of YouTube's news consumers (Shearer & Grieco, 2019). Those who get news on social media cite the convenience as the main reason for doing so, though a majority of them stated that they do not know why they consume news on social media (Shearer & Matsa, 2018). A large majority of adults say that social media sites treat some news organizations differently than others, giving preference to those that contain attention-grabbing headlines, that have large social media followings, and whose coverage has a particular political stance (Shearer & Grieco, 2019).

Beyond simply consuming news online, young adults are reacting to the news by using social media platforms as avenues for expressing political opinions and engaging in activism. In a late June 2020 survey, Pew Research Center found that a large majority of emerging adults use social media as a venue to express political opinions, state that social media is somewhat or very important when getting involved with political or social issues, and say social media are important for finding others who share their views, all of which have increased over 10% from 2018 (Auxier, 2020). This involves engaging in activity such as posting pictures to show support for a cause (42%), looking for information about local rallies and protests (54%), encouraging others to take action on issues that are important to them (44%), and using hashtags related to political or social issues (34%; Auxier, 2020).

How You Say It

The communication of emerging adults today is character-like of both the medium and their generational positions. As such, individuals born from 1995 to 2012 are known as members of the iGeneration (iGen; Twenge, 2014). Unique to the landscape of social media and digital technology use among iGen, "digitalk," a language that is abbreviated and not Standard written English, but is nonetheless purposeful and audience specific, efficient, inclusive, and personally expressive, adds another generational dimension to communication (Turner et al., 2014). As Gee and Hayes (2011) have pointed out, language online maintains aspects of oral language. For example, language online is also interactive. However, online technologies have made those interactions more complex and global, making the production and consumption of language exponential, and the multitasking requirements much more complex. Though oral language requires multitasking (e.g., listening, attending to the speaker, etc.), online communication demands much more complex management of language. The global nature of internet communication has seen the wide circulation of English and raised concerns about its dominance online engendering its lingua franca status (Christiansen, 2015).

Researchers have begun to examine college students' online communication to assess its uniqueness and consequent effects on such things as language apprehension, relationships, and lexical reliability. Entrenched in their everyday communication with peers, faculty, administrators, and family, digitalk (Turner et al., 2014) through textese (written language used in texting) that includes textisms (word abbreviations and emoticons; Lyddy et al., 2014) has declined since 2009. This decline may be a consequence of larger screens, easier keyboarding on mobile phones (Kemp & Grace, 2017), and the increase in character limits by communication apps such as Twitter (Larsen, 2017). Textisms are now often replaced by emojis, which are pictograms of real objects that can communicate affect by the sender (Riordan, 2017). Across all generations that have grown up in the digital age, images remain the most preferred type of content (Cox, 2019). Recognizing the shift by iGens to textese and away from Standard written English, researchers have found that textisms can have negative effects on students' reading and morphological awareness (De Jong & Kemp, 2012). The negative effects of social media on the communication and communication skills of iGens extend to concerns about selective exposure to content and perspectives narrowing their social ties (Kim & Kim, 2017); the impact of multitasking on devices while in the company of friends (Jacobsen & Forste, 2011); and the susceptibility to cyberbullying and racial assaults with an increase in time spent online (Gin et al., 2017; Machmutow et al., 2012).

There is ample research on the broader negative effects of social media on college students. McCready and colleagues (in press) have shown that racialized aggressions received by college students of color can negatively impact their mental health. Time spent on social media for nonacademic purposes (gaming, etc.) has been shown to negatively impact college students' grades (Lau, 2017). However, much of the research on social media's effects on college students suggests a greater likelihood that these media have positive effects on social support during the first year (De Andrea et al., 2012), persistence (Gray et al., 2013), and first-generation college goers' transition and engagement (Rowan-Kenyon et al., 2018).

Gender, racial identity, and generational differences also appear in studies of online communication. For example, college students are more likely than older adults to consider social media posts involving racism, sexism, and LGBTQ+ discrimination to be offensive (Wolfer, 2017). Though researchers have noted that the differences between predigital and digital generations may be a matter of familiarity and experience (Brown & Czerniewicz, 2010; Helsper & Eynon, 2010), unlike older digital immigrants who show a preference for asynchronous communication (email, Facebook), generations raised in the digital age prefer synchronous online communication (FaceTime, texting, group chats; Riordan et al., 2018). Women use emojis more and are more sensitive to negative emojis than men (Jones et al., 2020), while men tend to provide information and communicate negative emotions more frequently than women (Sun et al., 2020). Cross-cultural online communication between college peers has been shown to be influenced by cues on the student's ethnicity (student's name), altering the sender's lexicon on the email response (Hansen et al., 2015). However, studies have also shown that the use of emojis in online communication is recognized by students as a universal language (Kabir & Marlow, 2019), suggesting a lexical globalization and possibility of intercultural conversation. Racial identity has been shown to play a role in popular forms of social mobile use (e.g., texting, phone camera, and music), especially among women of color, and in general, belonging to a social identity group (e.g., racial, ethnic, gender) is the most significant attribute that is associated with frequently used mobile phone communication functionality (Barker, 2018). Understanding how multiple dimensions of identity are influenced by contextual influences, including social media, is a direction for future research (Abes et al., 2007).

Adapting to Student Communication Styles and Platforms

Students raised in the digital age communicate and receive information differently than prior generations of college students (e.g., Riordan et al., 2018). These students prefer electronic sources related to their educational experiences, including social media and other Web 2.0 technologies, because they expect rapid and efficient access to information (Rowan-Kenyon et al., 2016). Over the past two decades, higher education institutions have worked to evolve their communication strategies to better support the learning, needs, and interests of this population.

The importance of social media and recent generations begins before students ever set foot on their campuses. Social media serves as the primary source of information for iGen students during the college admissions process

(Rowan-Kenyon et al., 2018). Students also rely heavily on digital forms of communication to acclimate to their college communities prior to arriving to their institutions, and the peers they engage with online are pivotal to their college socialization (Martínez Alemán & Wartman, 2009). Higher education stakeholders can harness social media and text messaging to support iGen students during their college transitions. For example, Castleman and Page (2015) found that text message nudges used to inform underrepresented college-going students about prematriculation requirements led to increased enrollment of this population. Colleges and universities can actively use social media and other Web 2.0 technologies to engage prospective students and to onboard incoming students to their institutions.

Once iGen students begin their college experiences, they are increasingly willing to use social media and other online communication modalities to communicate with faculty and student service professionals (Gierdowski, 2019). Not only do students generally perceive that social media and other Web 2.0 technology usage in academic contexts is beneficial to their learning and helps to develop relationships with their peers and faculty (e.g., Delello et al., 2015), but also institutional online communication and Web 2.0–based resources can aid students as they navigate their time in college (Castleman & Meyer, 2020; Gierdowski, 2019) and benefit student outcomes (Rowan-Kenyon et al., 2016).

Some faculty continue to limit student use of social media and smartphone use in the classroom (Gierdowski, 2019), while others work to actively integrate these technologies into the curriculum (Rowan-Kenyon et al., 2016). The empirical findings related to social media and texting in the classroom are mixed. Many scholars support limiting technology in the classroom (e.g., Flanigan & Babchuk, 2015; Judd, 2014; Paul et al., 2012), as students who text in class may have lower grade point averages (GPAs) than their peers (Junco, 2012), and higher-frequency social media users self-report lower GPAs (Kirschner & Karpinski, 2010). Multitasking between course content and social media may take students' attention away from lessons and learning activities, negatively affecting student learning (Flanigan & Babchuk, 2015).

Others argue that social media and other Web 2.0 technologies can enrich course content and advance student outcomes. Faculty can use social media to connect external content to the in-class experience (Lowe & Laffey, 2011) and to foster relationships among learners and between the students and their instructors (Delello et al., 2015; Hamid et al., 2015). Learning activities that rely on social media and text messaging that is relevant to the course content may have positive effects on students' grades (Junco et al., 2011; Kuznekoff et al., 2015). As noted by Rowan-Kenyon et al. (2016), "Faculty's pedagogical investment in and creativity with social media appear to be key factors in their effectiveness as teaching and learning tools" (pp. 71–72), and the same may also be true with the intentional use of other Web 2.0 technologies in the classroom.

Regardless of the technology policies created by faculty, it is likely that students will continue to actively engage with social media and use their smartphones in the classroom. For example, 92% of students in a study conducted by Tindell and Bohlander (2012) reported that they texted during class, with a majority reporting that they believed their instructors were unaware of their smartphone use. Today's students are interested in using technology in the classroom, and they believe it can be used to enhance faculty and student relationships and to help them learn course content (Gierdowski, 2019). Prior to the COVID-19 pandemic, students reported that a majority of faculty allowed students to use laptops in the classroom, but only a quarter reported that faculty allowed in-class smartphone use (Gierdowski, 2019). Given the ubiquity of smartphone ownership by digital generations (Hitlin, 2018) and that these devices may be essential learning tools for this population, particularly students with fewer financial resources (Goldrick-Rab, 2018, tweet), faculty should provide students with greater latitude as to use of this technology in the classroom (Gierdowski, 2019).

Social media and Web 2.0 technologies are integral to students' social and cocurricular experiences, as student life and culture go beyond an institution's physical environment into the digital realm (Rowan-Kenyon et al., 2016). iGen students rely on social media and other digital forms of communication to acquire, maintain, and transmit social capital (Ellison et al., 2007) and to build, bridge, and reinforce peer relationships. This population is so reliant on social media and texting that they rarely, if at all, call or video conference with peers (Rowan-Kenyon et al., 2018). Because students' digital identities and behaviors are fundamental to their college experiences, student affairs professionals should leverage social media and other Web 2.0 technologies to support student learning and development (Junco, 2014). These educators can help students understand how self-presentation and digital identity affect outcomes and use digital communications as a cocurricular learning tool (Martínez Alemán & Wartman, 2009).

Student affairs professionals can also support iGen students as they navigate challenges encountered while communicating through social media and other technologies. Students must grapple with psychological stressors in the digital environment, such as anonymity on certain platforms, cyberbullying, and racial hostility, that affect their well-being, among other outcomes. While these challenges, and the speed with which they develop, can destabilize the student affairs practice (Rowan-Kenyon et al., 2016), student affairs practitioners must attend to the trauma students may face online. They must also be prepared to quickly adapt their practice in an ever-changing environment.

Student affairs professionals can also use social media, texting, and other technology to quickly deliver information to iGen students and to increase high-quality interactions among students and administrators (Junco, 2014). Creating compelling, accessible, and well-crafted social media campaigns continues to grow in importance in higher education, and student affairs professionals must continually assess their efforts to make the necessary adaptations to reach and engage their audience (Barnes, 2009). If student affairs professionals truly want to build bridges to foster student learning, they must actively engage students through digital communication (Junco, 2014).

While iGen students are willing to engage with their institutions on social media and other online communication modalities (e.g., text messaging), their expectations related to the content, style, and frequency of these messages differ greatly from their online communication with peers, family, and other social acquaintances. Taylor and Serna (2020) identified that the students preferred to receive one to three institutional text messages per week, and, to increase trustworthiness, these messages should include the students' names, identify the sender, and be devoid of slang. The participants also identified that they preferred messages focused on campus resources and deadlines, and they were less interested in messages containing course-related content. Student preferences related to institutional use of technology also varies across demographic groups (Rowan-Kenyon et al., 2016). For example, first-generation college students may limit their communication with faculty and staff to email for any official correspondence (Rowan-Kenyon et al., 2018). Faculty and other professionals interested in using social media and other online communication modalities to engage students must assess the online communication preferences of their students and conform their communication modalities and content to align with these preferences (Taylor & Serna, 2020).

If anything can be learned from educating during the COVID-19 pandemic, we must recognize that technology is a vital asset for student learning in higher education (O'Brien, 2020). Faculty and student affairs professionals must find ways to utilize social media and other forms of digital communication to promote student learning, development, and growth.

Conclusion

This chapter examined how emerging adults communicate differently than previous generations and the impacts on their communication capabilities. These differences include different modalities and platforms in the case of social media, along with the language that individuals are using to connect with others. Key ideas about adapting to student communication styles and platforms are included to help think about ways to promote student success. To further explore the application of this material, see the following case study along with guiding questions that faculty and student affairs professionals can utilize to discuss the case and think about ways to apply the chapter content to better support student success.

Case Study

As her alarm goes off on her iPhone telling her it is time to wake up and get ready for class, Sydney is excited and nervous. It is her first day of the fall semester at Millbrook University. As a first-generation Black college student, Sydney feels a great responsibility to her family to be successful, since they made a huge sacrifice for her to attend Millbrook. As she gets ready for class she gets a text from her mom: "U up? We ♡ U and Miss U!" She loves the message and types "miss u 2-FaceTime tonight!" At the same time, she gets a WhatsApp message from someone on her floor asking if anyone wants to get breakfast before class. "Yes—I don't have to face the cafeteria alone!" she thinks while responding, "B there in 10." She is thankful that her resident assistant created the WhatsApp group for them at their first floor meeting. As she finishes getting ready she watches a clip of Trevor Noah from *The Daily Show* about the upcoming election that was posted on Instagram by a friend from home.

After breakfast with four people from her floor, in which Jessica shared hilarious stories about attempting online dating over the summer, Sydney is off to her political science class with Dr. Poulson. A prelaw student, Sydney is most excited about this class and is looking forward to having engaging conversations with her peers. As class begins, she is slightly worried when Dr. Poulson walks in the room and declares that electronic devices are not to be used in class. "Oh no," she thinks, "I love to use my phone to look up quick facts or define words I don't know. What if I get an important text from my family?" As Sydney tries to put these thoughts out of her mind and attempts to focus, the professor asks what folks know about emerging details concerning one of the presidential candidates. "Ooh I know," she thinks and puts up her hand, along with a few other folks who timidly raise their hands. When Sydney is called on, she recalls the facts that she heard earlier from Trevor Noah. "Partially correct," responds Dr. Poulson. "Where did you learn this information?" "On Trevor Noah," she replies and hears nervous laughter around the classroom while Dr. Poulson dramatically hangs her head. "Why does no one read respected news sources anymore?" Dr. Poulson exclaims. "Oh no," thinks Sydney, "I am doomed in this class." The rest of the class goes by without incident, and as soon as it is over Sydney goes outside and gets on her phone. "How was class?" was the text from her older sister. "A disaster ☹ ☹ ☹ ☹," responds Sydney. "The professor thinks I am dumb."

At lunchtime, Sydney uses GroupMe to connect with four friends from her orientation group and walks through the First-Year Opportunity Fair during Millbrook's Welcome Week activities. The fair is very busy with hundreds of new students gathered on the campus quad for the afternoon festivities. Faculty, staff, and student leaders from offices and organizations stand behind tables advertising resources and ways to get involved on campus. Representatives encourage new students to sign up for listservs and many ask for Instagram usernames, Twitter handles, and cell phone numbers to be contacted via messaging apps. As a first-generation college student, Sydney was coached in her precollege program to get involved on campus in order to develop a peer network. As she walks through the fair, she feels more and more anxious. She gives her contact info to the Black Student Union and a few other organizations that her friends plan to join and she thinks to herself, "Do I really have to join these clubs if I can't find the club I want to get involved with? And will getting involved on campus take me away from the time that I could be spending each night connecting with my family back home?" Then she sees it: the Prelaw Society table. "Here is something that will be great to help me get to law school and make friends in my major!" She quickly signs up and provides all of her phone and social media contact information. As she talks to James, a student leader with the organization, she sees her Political Science professor coming toward them! James says, "Hi, let me introduce you to our advisor, Dr. Poulson." Embarrassed by her earlier class interaction, Sydney tries to make a quick exit when Dr. Poulson says to Sydney, "Thanks for speaking up in class today; email me to find a time so we can get to know each other better. I can share some good news sources with you." "OK," Sydney says and moves on to the next table. "That was weird," she thinks.

Later that day in her room, there is no one else around and she is lonely. She opens her school email account and is overwhelmed by the number of messages that are in there—not many seem important or personal to her. She has started to get texts from the clubs she signed up for earlier in the day announcing meeting times and locations; she has gotten regular texts, GroupMe messages, Facebook invites, and WhatsApp requests. As Sydney is scrolling through Snapchat she sees that she has been tagged in a picture that was posted by her best friend, Lisa. The photo is of the two of them the week before Sydney moved to Millbrook and the caption reads, "Miss and love U, hope your first day was great!" Sydney instantly feels homesick but sees Lisa is online and sends a quick Snap. The two chat for a few minutes, and Sydney tells Lisa about her day—the good and the bad. The two virtually chat for a few minutes about each other's weekends and how life is back at home. That night when she is Facetiming with her mom, she tells her about her interaction with her professor and the ups and downs of her day. Before they hang up, her mom says, "Before you go to bed you email that professor like she told you to do. She might be trying to help you." As she gets ready for bed, Sydney decides to write to Dr. Poulson.

Hi Dr. Poulson,

Hope U had a great day! ☺ Thanks for asking me to meet. Are you free tomorrow morning before noon, or after 5pm? If not, NBD-let me know what works for you.

Thanks,

Sydney

Guiding Questions

To connect the material in the chapter with practice, consider the following questions:

1. What are your thoughts on Sydney's first day of class? What are the strengths and missteps that you see here?
2. How can college and university administrators use their knowledge about current communication styles with this age group as a benefit to campus engagement and success?
3. What work do college and university faculty and staff need to do to help students with their current communication styles?

References

Abes, E. S., Jones, S. R., & McEwen, M. K. (2007). Reconceptualizing the model of multiple dimensions of identity: The role of meaning-making capacity in the construction of multiple identities. *Journal of College Student Development, 48*(1), 1–22. https://doi.org/10.1353/csd.2007.0000

Anderson, M., & Vogels, E. A. (2020, March 31). Americans turn to technology during COVID-19 outbreak, say an outage would be a problem. Pew Research Center. https://www.pewresearch.org/fact-tank/2020/03/31/americans-turn-to-technology-during-covid-19-outbreak-say-an-outage-would-be-a-problem/

Auxier, B. (2020, July 13). Americans' activism on social media differs by race, age, political party. Pew Research Center. https://www.pewresearch.org/fact-tank/2020/07/13/activism-on-social-media-varies-by-race-and-ethnicity-age-political-party/

Barker, V. (2018). Text you pictures: The role of group belonging, race identity, race, and gender in older adolescents' mobile phone use. *Social Sciences, 7*(7), 115. https://doi.org/10.3390/socsci7070115

Barnes, N. G. (2009). Reaching the wired generation: How social media is changing college admission. http://www.nacacnet.org/research/Publications Resources/Marketplace/discussion/Pages/SocialMediaDiscussionPaper.aspx

Brown, C., & Czerniewicz, L. (2010). Debunking the "digital native": Beyond digital apartheid, towards digital democracy. *Journal of Computer Assisted Learning, 26*(5), 357–369. https://doi.org/10.1111/j.1365-2729.2010.00369.x

Castleman, B. L., & Meyer, K. (2020). Can text message nudges improve academic outcomes in college? Evidence from a West Virginia initiative. *Review of Higher Education, 43*(4), 1125–1165. https://doi.org/10.1353/rhe.2020.0015

Castleman, B. L., & Page, L. C. (2015). Summer nudging: Can personalized text messages and peer mentor outreach increase college going among low-income high school graduates? *Journal of Economic Behavior & Organization, 115*, 144–160. doi:10.1016/j.jebo.2014.12.008

Christiansen, T. W. (2015). The rise of English as the global lingua franca. Is the world heading towards greater monolingualism or new forms of plurilingualism? *Lingue e Linguaggi, 15*, 129–154.

Cox, T. (2019, July 2). How different generations use social media. https://themanifest.com/social-media/how-different-generations-use-social-media

DeAndrea, D. C., Ellison, N. B., LaRose, R., Steinfield, C., & Fiore, A. (2012). Serious social media: On the use of social media for improving students' adjustment to college. *The Internet and Higher Education, 15*(1), 15–23.

De Jong, S., & Kemp, N. (2012). Text-message abbreviations and language skills in high school and university students. *Journal of Research & Reading, 35*(1), 49–68. https://doi.org/10.1111/j.1467-9817.2010.01466.x

Delello, J. A., McWhorter, R. R., & Camp, K. M. (2015). Using social media as a tool for learning: A multi-disciplinary study. *International Journal on E-Learning, 14*(2), 163–180.

Ellison, N. B., Steinfield, C., & Lampe, C. (2007). The benefits of Facebook friends: Social capital and college students' use of online social network sites. *Journal of Computer-Mediated Communication, 12*(4), 1143–1168. http://doi.org/10.1111/j.1083-6101.2007.00367.x

Flanigan, A. E., & Babchuk, W. A. (2015). Social media as academic quicksand: A phenomenological study of student experiences in and out of the classroom. *Learning and Individual Differences, 44*, 40–45. doi:10.1016/j.lindif.2015.11.003

Gee, J. P., & Hayes, E. R. (2011). *Language and learning in the digital age.* Routledge.

Gierdowski, D. C. (2019). *ECAR study of undergraduate students and information technology, 2019.* EDUCAUSE Center for Analysis and Research. https://library.educause.edu/-/media/files/library/2019/10/studentstudy2019.pdf?la=en&hash=25FBB396AE482FAC3B765862BA6B197DBC98B42C

Gin, K. J., Martínez-Alemán, A. M., Rowan-Kenyon, H. T., & Hottel, D. (2017). Social media and racialized aggressions on campus. *Journal of College Student Development, 58*(2), 159–174. https://doi.org/10.1353/csd.2017.0013

Goldrick-Rab, S. [@saragoldrickrab] (2018, December 1st). Moreover, I would love to see anyone attempt college these [Tweet]. Twitter https://twitter.com/saragoldrickrab/status/1068955957936431105

Gray, R., Vitak, J., Easton, E. W., & Ellison, N. B. (2013). Examining social adjustment to college in the age of social media: Factors influencing successful transitions and persistence. *Computers & Education, 67*, 193–207. https://doi.org/10.1016/j.compedu.2013.02.021

Hamid, S., Waycott, J., Kurnia, S., & Chang, S. (2015). Understanding students' perceptions of the benefits of online social networking use for teaching and learning. *Internet and Higher Education, 26*, 1–9. doi:10.1016/j.iheduc.2015.02.004

Hansen, M., Fabriz, S., & Stehle, S. (2015). Cultural cues in students' computer-mediated communication: Influences on e-mail style, perception of the sender, and willingness to help. *Journal of Computer-Mediated Communication, 20*(3), 278–294. https://doi.org/10.1111/jcc4.12110

Helsper, E. J., & Eynon, R. (2010). Digital natives: Where is the evidence? *British Educational Research Journal, 36*(3), 503–520. https://doi.org/10.1080/01411920902989227

Hitlin, P. (2018, September 28). Internet, social media use and device ownership in U.S. have plateaued after years of growth. Pew Research Center. https://www.pewresearch.org/fact-tank/2018/09/28/internet-social-media-use-and-device-ownership-in-u-s-have-plateaued-after-years-of-growth/

Jacobsen, W. C., & Forste, R. (2011). The wired generation: Academic and social outcomes of electronic media use among university students. *Cyberpsychology, Behavior, and Social Networking, 14*(5), 275–280. doi:10.1089/cyber.2010.0135

Jones, L. L., Wurm, L. H., Norville, G. A., & Mullins, K. L. (2020). Sex differences in emoji use, familiarity, and valence. *Computers in Human Behavior, 108*, 106305. https://doi.org/10.1016/j.chb.2020.106305

Judd, T. (2014). Making sense of multitasking: The role of Facebook. *Computers & Education, 70*, 194–202. doi:10.1016/j.compedu.2013.08.013

Junco, R. (2012). In-class multitasking and academic performance. *Computers in Human Behavior, 28*(6), 2236–2243. doi:10.1016/j.chb.2012.06.031

Junco, R. (2014). *Engaging students through social media: Evidence-based practices for use in student affairs*. Jossey-Bass.

Junco, R., Heiberger, G., & Loken, E. (2011). The effect of Twitter on college student engagement and grades. *Journal of Computer Assisted Learning, 27*(2), 119–132. doi:10.1111/j.1365-2729.2010.00387.

Kabir, H., & Marlow, D. W. (2019, July). Emojis in textual-based communication among college students: A study in perception and frequency. In *International Conference on Human-Computer Interaction* (pp. 336–344). Springer.

Kemp, N., & Grace, A. (2017). Txting across time: Undergraduates' use of "textese" in seven consecutive first-year psychology cohorts. *Writing Systems Research, 9*(1), 82–98. doi:10.1080/17586801.2017.1285220

Kim, B., & Kim, Y. (2017). College students' social media use and communication network heterogeneity: Implications for social capital and subjective well-being. *Computers in Human Behavior, 73*, 620–628. https://doi.org/10.1016/j.chb.2017.03.033

Kirschner, P. A., & Karpinski, A. C. (2010). Facebook and academic performance. *Computers in Human Behavior, 26*(6), 1237–1245. doi:10.1016/j.chb.2010.03.024

Kuznekoff, J. H., Munz, S., & Titsworth, S. (2015). Mobile phones in the classroom: Examining the effects of texting, Twitter, and message content on student learning. *Communication Education, 64*(3), 344–365. doi:10.1080/03634523.2015.1038727

Larsen, S. (2017, November 7). Welcome to a world with 280-character tweets. https://money.cnn.com/2017/11/07/technology/twitter-280-character-limit/index.html

Lau, W. W. (2017). Effects of social media usage and social media multitasking on the academic performance of university students. *Computers in Human Behavior, 68*, 286–291.

Lowe, B., & Laffey, D. (2011). Is Twitter for the birds?: Using Twitter to enhance student learning in a marketing course. *Journal of Marketing Education, 33*(2), 183–192. doi:10.1177/0273475311410851

Lyddy, F., Farina, F., Hanney, J., Farrell, L., & O'Neill, N. (2014). An analysis of language in university students' text messages. *Journal of Computer-Mediated Communication. 19*(3), 546–561. doi:10.1111/jcc4.12045.

Machmutow, K., Perren, S., Sticca, F., & Alsaker, F. (2012). Peer victimisation and depressive symptoms: Can specific coping strategies buffer the negative impact of cybervictimisation? *Emotional and Behavioral Difficulties, 17*(3–4), 403–420. https://doi.org/10.1080/13632752.2012.704310

Martínez Alemán, A. M., & Wartman, K. L. (2009). *Online social networking on campus: Understanding what matters in student culture.* Routledge.

McCready, A. M., Rowan-Kenyon, H. T., Martínez Alemán, A. M., & Barone, N. (2021). Students of color, mental health, and racialized aggressions on social media. *Journal of Student Affairs Research and Practice, 58*(2), 179–195.

Mitchell, A. (2018, December 3). Americans still prefer watching to reading the news—And mostly still through television. Pew Research Center. https://www.journalism.org/2018/12/03/americans-still-prefer-watching-to-reading-the-news-and-mostly-still-through-television/

O'Brien, J. (2020, May 5). More than a lifeline. *Inside Higher Ed.* https://www.insidehighered.com/views/2020/05/05/covid-19-has-demonstrated-how-technology-higher-ed-major-strategic-asset-opinion

Paul, J. A., Baker, H. M., & Cochran, J. D. (2012). Effect of online social networking on student academic performance. *Computers in Human Behavior, 28*(6), 2117–2127. doi:10.1016/j.chb.2012.06.016

Perrin, A., & Anderson, M. (2019). Share of U.S. adults using social media, including Facebook, is mostly unchanged since 2018. Pew Research Center. https://www.pewresearch.org/fact-tank/2019/04/10/share-of-u-s-adults-using-social-media-including-facebook-is-mostly-unchanged-since-2018/

Riordan, M. (2017). Emojis as tools for emotion work: Communicating affect in text messages. *Journal of Language and Social Psychology, 36*(5), 549–567. https://doi.org/10.1177/0261927X17704238

Riordan, M. A., Kreuz, R. J., & Blair, A. N. (2018). The digital divide: Conveying subtlety in online communication. *Journal of Computers in Education, 5*(1), 49–66. doi:10.1007/s40692-018-0100-6

Rowan-Kenyon, H. T., Martínez Alemán, A. M., Gin, K., Blakely, B., Gismondi, A., McCready, A., Lewis, J., Zepp, D., & Knight, S. A. (2016). Social media in higher education [Monograph]. *ASHE Higher Education Report, 42*, 5. John Wiley & Sons.

Rowan-Kenyon, H. T., Martínez Alemán, A. M., & Savitz-Romer, M. (2018). *Technology and engagement: Making technology work for first generation college students.* Rutgers University Press.

Shearer, E., & Grieco, E. (2019, October 2). Americans are wary of the role social media sites play in delivering the news. Pew Research Center. https://www.journalism.org/2019/10/02/americans-are-wary-of-the-role-social-media-sites-play-in-delivering-the-news/

Shearer, E., & Matsa, K. E. (2018, September 10). News use across social media platforms 2018. Pew Research Center. https://www.journalism.org/2018/09/10/news-use-across-social-media-platforms-2018/

Sun, B., Mao, H., & Yin, C. (2020). Male and female users' differences in online technology community based on text mining. *Frontiers in Psychology, 11*, 1–11. https://doi.org/10.3389/fpsyg.2020.00806

Taylor, Z. W., & Serna, K. L. (2020). Don't txt me l8r, text me now: Exploring community college student preferences for receiving a text message from their institution. *Community College Journal of Research and Practice, 44*(2), 133–146. https://doi.org/10.1080/10668926.2018.1560374

Tindell, D. R., & Bohlander, R. W. (2012). The use and abuse of cell phones and text messaging in the classroom: A survey of college students. *College Teaching, 60*(1), 1–9. doi:10.1080/87567555.2011.604802

Turner, K. H., Abrams, S. S., Katić, E., & Donovan, M. J. (2014). Demystifying digitalk: The what and why of the language teens use in digital writing. *Journal of Literacy Research, 46*(2), 157–193. https://doi.org/10.1177/1086296X14534061

Twenge, J. (2014). *Generation me-revised and updated: Why today's young Americans are more confident, assertive, entitled—and more miserable than ever before.* Simon and Schuster.

Wolfer, L. (2017). Age differences in online communication: How college students and adults compare in their perceptions of offensive Facebook posts. *Online Journal of Communication and Media Technologies, 7*(4), 24–42. https://doi.org/10.29333/ojcmt/2608

6

"You're My Person"

Building Meaningful Relationships with Emerging Adults

Thuha (Ha) Hoang and Lindsey (Ellen) Caillouet

Today's emerging adults are increasingly more diverse, not only in terms of race, ethnicity, age, socioeconomic levels, sexual orientation, geography, and enrollment status, but also in terms of expectations, intellectual capabilities, and interpersonal skills (Hussar et al., 2020). These diverse student populations pose new challenges to colleges and universities to create an integrated college experience that responds to the evolving needs of emerging adult learners from orientation to graduation. Connecting undergraduate experiences with learning, development, and relationships will build on existing institutional efforts to promote the success of all students.

For many emerging adults, the college years are an important growth period in which new relationships are sought as a means of developing their future adult lives and careers. They enter college with the idea that they will adjust to the demands of college life. Some individuals learn how to apply previously acquired relationship skills to new situations. Others are faced with the task of living alone for the first time and learning a new set of relationship skills appropriate for the intellectual and social norms of college life. For all, college is about finding meaningful relationships through interactions with parents, peers, faculty, and staff to support their path to adult attainment.

Transitions to New Relationships

The early college experience, for many emerging adults, marks the shift of moving from past communities associated with family, high school, and local residence to that of college (Tinto, 1993). It is the period where many find themselves between the old and new, especially for those who move away from their families and local residences. Too often, individuals must separate themselves from past relationships to make the transition to integrate

Thuha (Ha) Hoang and Lindsey (Ellen) Caillouet, *"You're My Person"* In: *Cultivating Student Success.* Edited by: Tisha A. Duncan and Allison A. Buskirk-Cohen, Oxford University Press. © Oxford University Press 2022. DOI: 10.1093/oso/9780197586693.003.0007 into college life. For all students, transitions to new social and academic relationships within their communities represent a complex sequence with multiple adjustments along with their college careers.

Past relationships differ from college in values, norms, behavioral, and intellectual characteristics that reflect a complex separation, in varying degrees, for individuals. For those who move away from their families to live at a distant college, the separation entails new stresses as the individual has to disassociate socially as well as physically. Others who attend local and nonresidential institutions may have less stress from separation but may not reap the benefits of their new relationships. For minority, first-generation, or disabled individuals, separation from the past may be isolating and difficult because they may not be familiar with institutional practices and often lack the personal networks for guidance (Padgett et al., 2012; Tinto, 1993). Reconstructing their daily lives can create a sense of conflicting identities that may strain relations with their past and new communities.

Movement from past associations to new communities represents a major shift in the expected course of emerging adults' relationships. In college, a student's sense of belonging, a feeling derived from the perception that one is an integral part of the community or institution, is an important factor in understanding relationships (Asher & Weeks, 2014). A sense of belonging, often linked to school affiliation, includes the individual's perceptions of *fit* and *value* at the same institution (Hagerty et al., 1992; Osterman, 2000). Underlying factors of belonging include a sense of one's abilities being recognized by others in the community and commitment to the institution and schoolwork, particularly academic work (Asher & Weeks, 2014). For belongingness, relationships are key factors that can contribute to the relative degree of fit and value in different contexts. A sense of belonging goes beyond just the quality of specific relationships but leads individuals to perceive a more global sense of belonging and feeling connected to the larger group or community.

For emerging adults, the college setting is an important site for opportunities in which to connect to the larger group. Across colleges, belongingness can facilitate many positive student outcomes (Gopalan & Brady, 2020; Pittman & Richmond, 2007, 2008; Walton & Brady, 2017). Individuals who perceive a strong social bond with others may engage more with their academic studies. Furthermore, a sense of belonging is positively linked to adjustment, scholastic competence, self-worth, mental health, and decreasing levels in internalizing behavior problems (Gopalan & Brady, 2020; Gummadam et al., 2016; Pittman & Richman, 2007, 2008). Individuals who have a trusting and interactive relationship with a teacher are more equipped to accept critical feedback and open to opportunities to learn (Cohen & Steele, 2002;

Freeman et al., 2007). Likewise, those who have favorable views of belonging are more likely to seek out and use campus resources (Gopalan & Brady, 2020; Strayhorn, 2012).

While most students feel that they belong at college, greater variability in belonging exists for underrepresented minority and first-generation students (Gopalan & Brady, 2020). At four-year colleges, underrepresented minority and first-generation students reported lower belonging than their peers. In academic settings, it has been suggested that individuals from minority groups feel an increased amount of belonging uncertainty (Fan et al., 2021; Walton & Cohen, 2007). When led to believe they had a low number of friends in a specific domain, minority students reported lower feelings of fit and potential in that domain. In contrast, when African American and Latino students were told they have social potential, their performance was lower on an IQ test (Skourletos et al., 2013). In the absence of a strong sense of belonging, an individual's own ethnic group may protect minority students who feel less connectedness to their college (Gummadam et al., 2016). Given the current educational structure, it is understandable for students from underrepresented populations to be sensitive to the real and potential quality of social bonds to help them "fit in" with their academic and social communities, a perception that can impact development, persistence, and outcomes.

Promoting Relationships Across the Institution

Starting in the critical first year, a student's sense of belonging contributes to engagement in the social system upon which subsequent faculty and peer relationships are built and established (Kuh et al., 2008; Tinto, 2012; Trolian et al., 2016). The social system, unlike the formal academic system, centers on the needs and daily life of the student. It comprises recurring interactions among students, peers, faculty, and staff that take place in hallways, cafeterias, residence halls, and other meeting places. While its activities emphasize the socialization component, the intellectual needs of the student may also be met during the interactions. The more students engage in formal or informal interactions with individuals on campus, especially with faculty, staff, and peers, the more likely they are to be satisfied with their first-year college experience and persist to the second year (Fischer, 2007). Subsequently, students who developed more relationships with faculty and peers during their first two years returned at a higher rate for their third year than those who departed college (Coghlan et al., 2010). The social system is likely to play an important role in a student's college experience and outcome. A sense of belonging contributes to meaningful relationships emerging adults have with parents, peers, and faculty and enhances their college experience. Though certain relationships may be more important for some students than others, such relationships support students' adjustment to the emotional, social, and academic demands of college life (Tinto, 2012).

Emerging Adult–Parent Relationships

Emerging adult–parent relationships are important to consider. While these influences are rarely analyzed through the frequency of contact students have with their parents, they are assessed using the status characteristics of parents. Factors such as parents' education level and occupations have been found to have positive influences on students' persistence in college and academic performance (DeFauw et al., 2018; Hussar et al., 2020). Parental involvement and encouragement are factors that also contribute to student success and development (Harper et al., 2012; Schwanz et al., 2014). Parents are often viewed to be more of an influence on student persistence than their peers (Boonk et al., 2018). Therefore, parental involvement should be fostered.

Social support or encouragement from family members impacts efforts in the formation and pursuit of their career choice. Parental support has been recognized as an important link to career outcomes, particularly for the career development of first-generation and ethnic minority students (Storlie et al., 2016; Westbrook & Scott, 2012). Positive relationships between parents and their children aided in developing open communication, responsibility, and desire to learn (DeFauw et al., 2018). Parental concern and encouragement helped students to select among the many options and choices encountered in their college experiences. Parents may also contribute to their children's abilities to overcome barriers as they gain a sense of confidence and skill in coping with the various personal and educational barriers (Raque-Bogdan et al., 2013).

Student-Peer Relationships

Peer relationships offer unique experiences for emerging adults. These experiences are often voluntary, egalitarian, and complementary, unlike experiences shared with family members (Rubin et al., 2015). Peer relations refer to "a broad set of direct and indirect experiences that individuals of all ages have with their nonfamilial age-mates" (Rubin et al., 2015, p. 325). Peer relationships offer unique yet complex socialization experiences, both positive and negative. For instance, peer relationships involving emotionally and socially competent individuals can act as protective measures for peer group members (Maunder & Monks, 2019). On the other hand, constructs such as rejection, victimization, and exclusion might lead to negative consequences (Chen & Rubin, 2011). Therefore, the quality of peer relationships is a significant factor impacting the subsequent development and adjustment of emerging adults within the larger social and academic systems.

Peer relationships can influence students in myriad ways. Because both acceptance and approval are key attributes, conforming to group norms and beliefs is commonplace. Peer modeling of behaviors such as studying, learning, intellectual development, and the desire to obtain careers requiring a college degree strongly influence student persistence and attrition (Bank et al., 1990). Students who feel more closely connected with their peers want them to be successful academically; therefore, they may positively influence their academic performance and satisfaction with the college experience (Bank et al., 1990; Goguen et al., 2011). Being active participants in campus activities with peers may also increase their grade point averages (Goguen et al., 2011). They also have a greater sense of belonging to the university as a whole because they feel as though their involvement in the campus environment is valued (Buskirk-Cohen & Plants, 2019). Furthermore, students' sense of belonging is increased when they feel valued, supported, and respected by their peers (Zumbrunn et al., 2014). In contrast, students who do not feel accepted among their peers have feelings of indifference toward them. This may elicit negative feelings of embarrassment and disengagement when working with their peers in classroom settings because they believe they lack the skills to work cooperatively (Zumbrunn et al., 2014).

Additionally, friends and peers influence emerging adults as they make career choices and decisions. Peer support was found to be related to positive academic experiences in high school and college and a noted source to cope with career development barriers (Dennis et al., 2005; Lent et al., 2002). First-generation students view their peers as more equipped than family to provide the needed support and instruction to do well in college (Dennis et al., 2005). However, friends can also have a negative influence on one's career choice and development. At-risk students who are surrounded by friends who lack focus on their future careers will likely experience more conflict surrounding their career choice, development, and decision-making skills (Horton, 2015).

Student-Faculty Relationships

While parents and peers both play significant roles, the relationships students form with faculty greatly influence their college experiences (Bank et al., 1990; Komarraju et al., 2010; Lundberg & Schreiner, 2004; Trolian et al., 2016; Wang et al., 2014). Formal interactions students have with faculty contribute to the formation of meaningful relationships. Discussions may be limited to academic and vocational advising and mentoring, focusing primarily on intellectual considerations within classroom settings (Komarraju et al., 2010). Formal interactions students have with faculty may have a greater impact on academic achievement and overall satisfaction with their education (Loes & Pascarella, 2015).

Formal interactions between students and faculty may also positively influence students' confidence. Traditional faculty advising influences students' social self-confidence positively and can lead to several positive outcomes (Workman, 2015). For instance, students may be more willing to approach faculty on both informal and formal levels. Students who view approaching faculty as less psychologically threatening may do so more often (Loes & Pascarella, 2015). These students are also more likely to have better interpersonal skills. Furthermore, faculty who are more helpful and provide quality advising can potentially increase students' satisfaction with education (Workman, 2015). First-year advising programs of staff and faculty help early social and academic integration (Workman, 2015). Effective advising programs such as these can increase not only student satisfaction but also persistence.

Additionally, formal interactions between students and faculty help students feel more connected to their instructors and peers. Instructors have a notable impact on providing students with a sense of belonging through the instructional design of their course (Buskirk-Cohen & Plants, 2019). Instructors who set a positive tone for the class, demonstrate enthusiasm, and promote peer collaboration often help students feel valued in the classroom community (Webber et al., 2013; Zumbrunn et al., 2014). Encouraging productive group work will help students feel more supported. Furthermore, when the course content is meaningful and relevant, student engagement and feelings of belonging increase. Emphasizing the importance of respect also helps to create a safe and positive environment where student interaction and participation are encouraged (Buskirk-Cohen & Plants, 2019; Zumbrunn et al., 2014). In contrast, students who do not establish a healthy sense of belonging will often feel uncomfortable and less engaged in the classroom.

Informal student-faculty interactions involve more personal relationships outside of the classroom, thus developing stronger bonds to faculty and the college (Komarraju et al., 2010). Close and personal connections between faculty and students are associated with greater college persistence and emotional and cognitive growth (Li et al., 2011). However, faculty are less influential than peers and parents when considering attrition (Bank et al., 1990). Other benefits associated with informal student-faculty interactions involve greater self-motivation and academic performance of students (Komarraju et al., 2010).

One main predictor concerning the extent to which informal student-faculty interaction occurs is the level of students' self-esteem and confidence (Komarraju et al., 2010). Confident students feel less threatened when approaching faculty. Students' sense of belonging is also increased when instructors are more approachable and available in and outside of the classroom (Zumbrunn et al., 2014). Therefore, faculty need to understand the importance of informal interactions and encourage communication on a personal level with students. Students should also be more persistent in their involvement with faculty outside of classroom settings, such as face-to-face advising to help with their transition to college and decision-making processes (Workman, 2015). Colleges and universities should consider ways to improve the quality of student-faculty interactions, such as reconstructing academic advising and developing opportunities for students and faculty to interact through departmental or institutional programs designed to encourage meaningful discussions (Bank et al., 1990; Trolian et al., 2016). Due to the increase in diverse student populations, it is crucial for faculty to approach ethnic minority students who perhaps may find it difficult to approach them (Komarraju et al., 2010).

A student's sense of purpose is fostered when both formal and informal student-faculty interactions are frequent; however, this is not merely enough (Trolian et al., 2016). Both the quality and frequency of these interactions greatly impact students' academic motivation, learning, and effort, thus contributing to their sense of purpose (Lundberg & Schreiner, 2004; Trolian et al., 2016). The likelihood of students forming quality relationships with faculty members depends on if they perceive their faculty members as being approachable, caring, enthusiastic, and available for frequent interactions outside of the classroom (Komarraju et al., 2010). Perhaps the most significant quality is respect. Students who perceive faculty as being genuinely respectful toward them are more likely to form meaningful, informal relationships (Komarraju et al., 2010). Often, students value the time faculty spend with them out of the classroom (Komarraju et al., 2010; Trolian et al., 2016). This is particularly relevant to students who may be from first-generation, minority, or disadvantaged backgrounds because these students now have an additional resource to rely on for professional guidance and career development (Komarraju et al., 2010).

Faculty support may influence a student's career goals and create a greater sense of belonging. Students believe their instructors are more invested in their academic success because of their supportive and respectful nature (Zumbrunn et al., 2014). Faculty who express interest and support for students' career plans help to reinforce the pursuit of certain academic subjects and attitudes toward professional success (Trolian et al., 2020). When faculty engage in positive interactions, students in return perceive competence and abilities to meet academic expectations. Faculty can serve as role models in career choice by exploration in and outside the classroom. Working with industry experts in the local community provides students with work-based learning experiences such as career exploration fairs, job shadowing, field trips, and internships. Experiences in occupational fields and tasks influence students' expected choices and commitment (Lent et al., 2002). When faculty and career planning services collaborate to provide a wide range of career-oriented learning experiences, students may be able to pursue their career options.

The present view of belongingness places great stress on the actions of various individuals who support students. Support and assistance from family, peers, and faculty provide a protective factor against stresses and promote social integration (Asher & Weeks, 2014). However, deficits in social bonds impact motivation, emotional well-being, stress, coping, and happiness (Baumeister & Leary, 1995). For some, deficiencies (actual or perceived) in an individual's social relationships may lead students to experience transient loneliness. Furthermore, chronic loneliness has been related to a wide range of negative psychological and health outcomes, including depression (Fontaine et al., 2009; Kumaraswamy, 2012) and poorer immune health (Pressman et al., 2005). Due to their emotional vulnerability state, some may bond with delinquent peers, join gangs, and engage in group violence (O'Brien et al., 2012; Turpin-Petrosino, 2002).

Conclusion

Meaningful relationships do not occur overnight. Rather, they often take several years of development and assessments, in which administration, faculty, and staff work together on content and experiences reflecting the needs of students from entry to the final phase of their studies. Beginning with the institution, fundamental conversations between administration, faculty, and staff may start with the rarely asked questions: What is the purpose of relationships for first-year students? Beyond the first year, how do we promote relationships that will lead to student success and program completion?

As more individuals from different backgrounds, experiences, and abilities seek postsecondary education, the challenge for all will be to understand the complex and dynamic relationship process that draws from a variety of contemporary sources and contextual factors. For many, access to supportive conditions helps students' learning environments on and off campus. Clearly, opportunities across classrooms and campus that stress meaningful relationships as central to learning, development, and success increase students' capacity for academic and institutional life and beyond.

Case Study

Carlos, age 18, graduated with a 3.25 grade point average from a public high school. He will be attending a local, public university in the fall, majoring in general business, and will be living on campus. Having spent K–12th grade in a local public school system, he is eager yet apprehensive about attending a four-year public college. This is the first time that he will be living on his own, leaving his parents and four younger siblings. While his parents are proud of his accomplishments, they also are unsure of his success in college. Both parents attended high school; however, only his mother graduated. His father works in the public works department for the city government, while his mother is an accountant for a local restaurant. They both want Carlos to be independent and successful. Carlos shares the following:

> I am very nervous about being on my own and not having my parents there when I need them. I know they have worked hard to get me here, working nights and weekends. They made so many sacrifices. I don't want to let my family down.

It is the second half of the first semester being away from home. Carlos has made few friends and feels like an outsider. While he attends all of his classes, he is reluctant to speak up in class out of fear of being judged. He has not socialized outside of the classroom either. He called home expressing his feelings to his parents. Throughout elementary, middle, and high school, Carlos has typically been a B student. He has a strong work ethic and wants to be successful academically. However, he has found himself struggling during his first semester. He is making mostly Cs in his classes. He is feeling discouraged and questioning if college is even right for him. Due to feelings of loneliness and academic challenges, Carlos is struggling with maintaining self-confidence and motivation. He often feels like he wants to give up but is often reminded of his parents' many sacrifices. He knows that he needs help but is unsure whom he should turn to.

Consider this discussion on developing meaningful relationships to help Carlos overcome these challenges. The goal is to assist Carlos with his transition while also creating your own solutions and accessing the available resources of your institution.

Guiding Questions

1. What suggestions might help Carlos overcome feelings of isolation?
2. What are ways the institution could promote Carlos's relationships with peers and faculty?
3. What are ways faculty could help Carlos with his academic struggles both inside and outside the classroom?
4. In what other ways will Carlos's relationships with faculty and/or staff help with his self-confidence and motivation?

References

Asher, S. R., & Weeks, M. S. (2014). Loneliness and belongingness in the college years. In R. Coplan & J. C. Bowker (Eds.), *The handbook of solitude psychological perspectives on social isolation, social withdrawal, and being alone* (pp. 283–301). John Wiley & Sons.

Bank, B. J., Slavings, R. L., & Biddle, B. J. (1990). Effects of peer, faculty, and parental influences on students' persistence. *American Sociological Association, 63*(3), 208–225.

Baumeister, R. F., & Leary, M. R. (1995). The need to belong: Desire for interpersonal attachments as a fundamental human motivation. *Psychological Bulletin, 117*(3), 497–529.

Boonk, L., Gijselaers, H. J. M., Ritzen, H., & Brand-Gruwel, S. (2018). A review of the relationship between parental involvement indicators and academic achievement. *Educational Research Review, 24*, 10–30.

Buskirk-Cohen, A. A., & Plants, A. (2019). Caring about success: Students' perceptions of professors' caring matters more than grit. *International Journal of Teaching and Learning in Higher Education, 31*(1), 108–114.

Chen, X., & Rubin, K. (2011). *Socioemotional development in cultural context.* Guilford Press.

Coghlan, C., Fowler, J., & Messel, M. (2010). *The sophomore experience: Identifying factors related to second-year attrition.* Paper presented at the annual meeting of the Consortium for Student Retention Data Exchange, Mobile.

Cohen, G. L., & Steele, C. M. (2002). A barrier of mistrust: How stereotypes affect cross- race mentoring. In J. Aronson (Ed.), *Improving academic achievement: Impact of psychological factors on education*. Academic Press.

DeFauw, C., Levering, K., Msipa, R. T., & Abraham, S. (2018). Families' support and influence on college students' educational performance. *Journal of Education and Development*, 2(1). 11–19.

Dennis, J. M., Phinney, J. S., & Chuateco, L. I. (2005). The role of motivation, parental support, and peer support in academic success of ethnic minority first-generation college students. *Journal of College Student Development*, 46(3), 223–236.

Fan, X., Luchok, K., & Dozier, J. (2020). College students' satisfaction and sense of belonging: Differences between underrepresented groups and the majority groups. *SN Social Sciences, 1*, 22. https://doi.org/10.1007/s43545-020-00026-0

Fischer, M. (2007). Settling into campus life: Differences by race/ethnicity in college involvement and outcomes. *Journal of Higher Education*, 78(2), 126–161.

Fontaine, R. G., Yang, C., Burks, V. S., Dodge, K. A., Price, J. M., Pettit, G. S., & Bates, J. E. (2009). Loneliness as a partial mediator of the relation between low social preference in childhood and anxious/depressed symptoms in adolescence. *Development and Psychopathology, 21*, 479–491.

Freeman, T. M., Anderman, L. H., & Jensen, J. M. (2007). Sense of belonging in college freshman at the classroom and campus levels. *Journal of Experimental Education*, 75(3), 203–220.

Goguen, L. M., Hiester, M. A., & Nordstrom, A. H. (2011). Associations among peer relationships, academic achievement, and persistence in college. *College Student Retention, 12*(3), 319–337.

Gopalan, M., & Brady, S. T. (2020). College students' sense of belonging: A national perspective. *Educational Researcher*, 49(2), 134–137.

Gummadam, P., Pittman, L. D., & Ioffe, M. (2016). School belonging ethnic identity, and psychological adjustment among ethnic minority college students. *Journal of Experimental Education*, 84(2), 289–306.

Hagerty, B. M. K., Lynch-Sauer, J., Patusky, K. L., Bouwsema, M., & Collier, P. (1992). Sense of belonging: A vital mental health concept. *Archives of Psychiatric Nursing, 6*, 172–177.

Harper, C. E., Sax, L. J., & Wolf, D. S. (2012). The role of parents in college students' sociopolitical awareness, academic, and social development. *Journal of Student Affairs Research and Practice*, 49(2), 137–156.

Horton, J. (2015). Identifying at-risk factors that affect college student success. *International Journal of Process Education*, 7(1), 83–101.

Hussar, B., Zhang, J., Hein, S., Wang, K., Roberts, A., Cui, J., Smith, M., Bullock Mann, F., Barmer, A., & Dilig, R. (2020). *The condition of education 2020* (NCES 2020-144). U.S. Department of Education, National Center for Education Statistics. https://nces.ed.gov/pubsearch/pubsinfo.asp?pubid=2020144

Komarraju, M., Musulkin, S., & Bhattacharya, G. (2010). Role of student-faculty interactions in developing college students' academic self-concept, motivation, and achievement. *Journal of College Student Development*, 51(3), 332–342.

Kuh, G. D., Cruce, T. M., Shoup, R., & Kinzie, J. (2008). Unmasking the effects of student engagement on first-year college grades and persistence. *Journal of Higher Education, 79*(5), 540–563.

Kumaraswamy, N. (2012). Academic stress, anxiety and depression among college-students: A brief review. *International Review of Social Sciences and Humanities*, 5(1), 135–143.

Lent, R. W., Brown, S. D., Talleyrand, R., McPartland, E. B., Davis, T., Chopra S. B., Alexander, B. S., Suthakaran, V., & Chai C. (2002). Career choice barriers, supports, and coping strategies: College students' experiences. *Journal of Vocational Behavior*, 60(1), 61–72.

Li, L., Pitts, J. P., & Finley, J. (2011). Which is a better choice for student-faculty interaction: Synchronous or asynchronous communication? *Journal of Technology Research*, *2*(1), 1–12.

Loes, C. N., & Pascarella, E. T. (2015). The benefits of good teaching extend beyond course achievement. *Journal of the Scholarship of Teaching and Learning*, *15*(2), 1–13.

Lundberg, C. A., & Schreiner, L. A. (2004). Quality and frequency of faculty-student interaction as predictors of learning: An analysis by student race/ethnicity. *Journal of College Student Development*, *45*(5), 549–565.

Maunder, R., & Monks, C. (2019). Friendships in middle childhood: Links to peer and school identification, and general self-worth. *British Journal of Developmental Psychology*, *37*(1), 211–299.

O'Brien, K., Daffern, M., Chu, C. M., & Thomas, S. (2012). Youth gang affiliation, violence, and criminal activities: A review of motivational, risk, and protective factors. *Aggression and Violent Behavior*, *18*, 417–425.

Osterman, K. F. (2000). Students' need for belonging in the school community. *Review of Educational Research*, *70*(3), 323–367.

Padgett, R. D., Johnson, M. P., & Pascarella, E. T. (2012). First-generation undergraduate students and the impacts of the first year college: Additional evidence. *Journal of College Student Development*, *53*(2), 243–266.

Pittman, L. D., & Richmond, A. (2007). Academic and psychological functioning in late adolescence: The importance of school belonging. *Journal of Experimental Education*, *75*(4), 270–290.

Pittman, L. D., & Richmond, A. (2008). University belonging, friendship quality, and psychological adjustment during the transition to college. *Journal of Experimental Education*, *76*(4), 343–361.

Pressman, S. D., Cohen, S., Miller, G. E., Barkin, A., Rabin, B. S., & Treanor, J. J. (2005). Loneliness, social network size, and immune response to influenza vaccination in college freshmen. *Health Psychology*, *24*, 297–306.

Raque-Bogdan, T. L., Klingaman, E. A., Martin, H. M., & Lucas, M. S. (2013). Career-related parent support and career barriers: An investigation of contextual variables. *Career Development Quarterly*, *61*(4), 339–353.

Rubin, K., Bukowski, W., & Bowker, J. (2015). Children in peer groups. In M. Bornstein, T. Leventhal, & R. Lerner (Eds.), *Handbook of child psychology and development science: Ecological settings and processes* (pp. 175–222). John Wiley & Sons.

Schwanz, K. A., Palm, L. J., Hill-Chapman, C. R., & Broughton, S. F. (2014). College students' perceptions of relations with parents and academic performance. *American Journal of Educational Research*, *2*(1), 13–17.

Skourletos, J. C., Murphy, M. C., Emerson, K. T., & Carter, E. A. (2013). Social identity and academic belonging: Creating environments to minimize the achievement gap among African American and Latino students. *Psychological Studies*, *18*(2), 23–29.

Storlie, C. A., Mostade, S. J., & Duenyas, D. (2016). Cultural trailblazer: Exploring the career development of Latina first-generation college students. *Career Development Quarterly*, *64*, 304–317.

Strayhorn, T. L. (2012). *College students' sense of belonging: A key to educational success for all students*. Routledge.

Tinto, V. (1993). *Leaving college: Rethinking the causes and cures of student attrition*. University of Chicago Press.

Tinto, V. (2012). *Completing college: Rethinking institutional action*. University of Chicago Press.

Trolian, T. L., Jach, E. A., & Archibald, G. C. (2020). Shaping students' career attitudes toward professional success: Examining the role of student-faculty interactions. *Innovative Higher Education*, *46*(2), 111–131. https://doi.org/10.1007/s10755-020-09529-3

Trolian, T. L., Jach, E. A., Hanson, J. A., & Pascarella, E. T. (2016). Influencing academic motivation: The effects of student-faculty interaction. *Journal of College Student Development, 57*(7), 810–826.

Turpin-Petrosino, C. (2002). Hateful sirens. . . Who hears their song? An examination of student attitudes toward hate groups and affiliation potential. *Journal of Social Issues, 58*(2), 281–301.

Walton, G. M., & Brady, S. T. (2017). The many questions of belonging. In A. J. Elliot, C. S. Dweck, & D. S. Yeager (Eds.), *Handbook of competence and motivation: Theory and application* (2nd ed.). Guilford Press.

Walton, G. M., & Cohen, G. L. (2007). A question of belonging: Race, social fit, and achievement. *Journal of Personality and Social Psychology, 92*(1), 82–96.

Wang, J. S., Laird, T. F., Pascarella, E., & Ribera, A. (2015). How clear and organized classroom instruction and deep approaches to learning affect growth in critical thinking and need for cognition. *Studies in Higher Education, 40*(10), 1786–1807.

Webber, K. L., Krylow, R. B., & Zhang, Q. (2013). Does involvement really matter? Indicators of college student success and satisfaction. *Journal of College Development, 54*(6), 591–611.

Westbrook, S. B., & Scott, J. A. (2012). The influence of parents on the persistence decisions of first-generation college students. *Focus on Colleges, Universities, and Schools, 6*(1), 1–9.

Workman, J. L. (2015). Exploratory students' experiences with first-year academic advising. *NACADA, 35*(1), 5–12.

Zumbrunn, S., McKim, C., Buhs, E., & Hawley, L. R. (2014). Support, belonging, motivation, and engagement in the college classroom: A mixed method study. *Instructional Science, 42*(5), 661–684.

7

"I've Never Had to Do This on My Own"

Support to Address Retention and Success for Emerging Adults

Kevin Correa and Sylvia Symonds

As Tinto (2008) has so eloquently noted, "access without support is not opportunity." Researchers have argued that colleges and universities must commit to and prioritize student success and retention programs with financial and human resources (Engle & Tinto, 2008). Student success outcomes, including retention and graduation, must be part of an overall strategy that is intentional, embraced, incentivized, and proactive by faculty, staff, and students (Engle & O'Brien, 2007; Pike & Kuh, 2005). With decreasing numbers of high school graduates in the college pipeline (Bransberger & Michelau, 2016), colleges and universities are focusing on improving student success outcomes, including transition and integration for those students who opt to pursue higher education. For many decades, colleges and universities have focused on retaining students into their second year; however, only in recent years have they examined how student success and retention strategies influence specific groups, including low-income students, first-generation students, students of color, and out-of-state students (Correa, 2017). Given the increasing number of first-generation students pursuing higher education (Cardoza, 2016), it is not surprising that practitioners, scholars, colleges, and universities are paying closer attention to this and other groups. Given this context, colleges and universities have implemented a variety of programs and strategies to increase student success outcomes for students.

As part of their strategic retention efforts, some colleges and universities are using programs and initiatives that focus on building students' academic skills. Although academic preparation is an essential element of student success, research suggests that up to 75% of all decisions to drop out are motivated by nonacademic reasons, which leads researchers to suggest that efforts to increase retention should be focused on other parts of the student experience beyond academics (Tinto, 1999). Other factors that have been found

Kevin Correa and Sylvia Symonds, *"I've Never Had to Do This on My Own"* In: *Cultivating Student Success*. Edited by: Tisha A. Duncan and Allison A. Buskirk-Cohen, Oxford University Press. © Oxford University Press 2022.
DOI: 10.1093/oso/9780197586693.003.0008

to play a role in student retention and success include personal and environmental conditions (Bean & Metzner, 1985; Tinto, 1993). Though not exhaustive, these factors provide a framework to consider widely implemented higher education policies designed to impact retention.

First-Generation Students

Almost one-third of students entering two- or four-year colleges are the first in their families to graduate from college (Cardoza, 2016). Although first-generation students enroll in substantial numbers, they are less likely to continue on their postsecondary pathway. Three years after first enrolling, the National Center for Educational Statistics reported that 33% of first-generation students had left their postsecondary program of study compared to 14% of students with parents who have completed at least a bachelor's degree, also known as continuing-generation students (Cataldi et al., 2018). The same report highlighted a similar gap when looking at six-year graduation rates: 56% of first-generation students had obtained a credential or remained enrolled compared to 74% of continuing-generation students (Cataldi et al., 2018).

Some of these gaps may be explained by the many ways colleges and universities presume a level of familiarity with college knowledge, which includes

> an understanding of the following processes: college admissions including curricular, testing, and application requirements; college options and choices, including the tiered nature of postsecondary education; tuition costs and the financial aid system; placement requirements, testing, and standards; the culture of college; and the challenge level of college courses, including increasing expectations of higher education. (Conley, 2007, p. conley17)

Many students, including first-generation students, may not be familiar with elements of college knowledge. This knowledge, which has also been called the hidden curriculum, is defined as "the mix of bureaucratic know-how and sound study skills that can make or break a student's first year in college". (Zinshteyn, 2016, para. 5). Colleges and universities have pursued various strategies designed to teach information and skills essential for a successful college student, including financial aid, student engagement, study habits, and other skills (Education Advisory Board [EAB], 2016).

Research indicates that students benefit from finding a place on campus where they can connect with peers from similar backgrounds and share what they have learned about navigating the challenges they experience by being low-income or first-generation college students (Engle & O'Brien, 2007; Muraskin, 1997). Making a connection with an advisor, peer, or faculty member is a positive indicator of undergraduate student success (Kuh et al., 2006). Indeed, Kuh et al. (2006) argued, "The single best predictor of student satisfaction with college is the degree to which they perceive the college environment to be supportive of their academic and social needs" (p. 40). Furthermore, a student's ability to make a meaningful connection with a member of the university community is one important predictor of student persistence (Pike & Kuh, 2005). This chapter will offer a brief overview of advising and mentoring, highlight the literature related to peer coaching, and conclude with a case study and guiding questions for institutions and practitioners who are considering this approach to student success.

Advising and Mentoring in Higher Education

Academic advising is a prime example of how colleges and universities help students navigate the higher education environment. While the goals of advising are multifaceted, advising is often intended to support students in selecting their courses, understanding degree requirements, and making the connection between their academic choices and larger goals (Mu & Fosnacht, 2019). A national study of 156 colleges and universities found that advising experiences have a positive relationship with students' grades and self-perceived gains (Mu & Fosnacht, 2019). Research has demonstrated a connection between advising to targeted groups via approaches like specialized advising offices and increases in retention rates (Bean & Metzner, 1985; Braxton et al., 2007). Some assert academic advisors are uniquely suited to meet the needs of college students because of their own educational experiences (White & Schulenberg, 2012). There are numerous approaches to advising, and newer approaches such as appreciative advising, strengths-based advising, and advising informed by self-authorship have emerged in recent years (Drake et al., 2013).

In addition to advisors, faculty members play an essential role as the "major agents of socialization" (Pascarella et al., 1994, p. 31) concerning a student's experience on campus. Studies have demonstrated the benefits of these interactions, leading to the recommendation that every student should strive to get to know at least one faculty member every semester (Light, 2001). This recommendation places the onus on the student to seek out the faculty member. That seems unlikely to happen when one study revealed that only

20% of students had spoken to faculty outside of the classroom setting, and 75% of students agreed that contact with faculty outside of class was minimal (Hagedorn et al., 2000). Additional research found that only 50% of college students had ever contacted a faculty member outside of class (Jaasma & Koper, 1999). More recent research has found that frequency of faculty-student interactions varies by race, gender, social class, and first-generation status, with first-generation college students having much less interaction (Kim & Sax, 2009). Lack of student-faculty interaction is unfortunate because more personal and intentional faculty-student interactions are beneficial for students in many ways, including student learning outcomes, integration into college life, and student retention (Hurtado & Carter, 1997; Milem & Berger, 1997). Positive faculty-student interactions can also foster students' sense of belonging (Malm et al., 2020).

A final strategy we feel is worth highlighting is mentoring. Research has indicated that students find mentoring to be valuable (Smith, 2009), and Latino students in particular report a higher-quality student experience and an increased likelihood of persisting in their third year after participating in a mentoring program (Torres & Hernandez, 2009). The literature focused on the impact of mentoring on students more generally finds it has a significant and positive relationship to retention (Campbell & Campbell, 1997; Mangold et al., 2003; Pagan & Edwards-Wilson, 2003; Salinitri, 2005). In practice, many individuals can serve in a mentoring role, including faculty, college or university staff, religious leaders, more senior students, graduate students, alumni, and undergraduate peers (Crisp & Cruz, 2009; Zalaquett & Lopez, 2006). In particular, mentoring conducted by faculty members has many benefits for students (Ishiyama, 2007). Mentoring relationships can be formal or informal, variable in duration, and intentional or unplanned (Luna & Cullen, 1995). More informal or spontaneous mentoring may not be overseen or sanctioned by the higher education institution and tends to be more focused on a specific goal. For instance, an undergraduate student might ask a faculty member to give them guidance on how to get into graduate school (Campbell & Campbell, 1997). Formal mentoring relationships are likely to be sponsored or sanctioned by the higher education institution and typically are assigned by program staff or someone else outside of the mentor/mentee relationship (Crisp & Cruz, 2009).

In addition to mentoring provided by staff and faculty, several more recent studies revealed increasing trends of using undergraduate students in a peer mentoring capacity (Gershenfeld, 2014). Other peer education opportunities led by college students include tutoring, supplemental instruction, academic advisement, health education, first-year seminars, and coaching (Latino &

Unite, 2012). Increasingly, colleges and universities are incorporating some peer mentoring programs or components into institutional student success and retention strategies, demonstrating that peer mentoring has become a national priority and a valued student success practice (Girves et al., 2005). As will be discussed in further detail, coaching draws upon some elements embraced by other student success approaches, including an individualized student approach, fostering relationships between students and others on campus, and taking account of both the academic and social needs of students when developing support services.

Coaching in Higher Education

One more recent approach college and university leaders have pursued as a student success strategy is coaching (Hayes, 2012; Robinson & Gahagan, 2010). Coaching was initially introduced to higher education when the service provider InsideTrack offered it as a means of increasing student retention (Bettinger & Baker, 2011). In the intervening years, various models of coaching have been embraced by hundreds of colleges and universities across the United States, including those using peer coaches. Given that coaching is a relatively new service offered to college students, there is considerably less research on its impact on student success outcomes, including retention. Researchers who conducted the most comprehensive study to date indicating coaching is having a positive impact on student success contended that additional research is warranted, particularly concerning how the specific characteristics of coaches influence their efficacy (Bettinger & Baker, 2011).

In the simplest terms, coaching involves "using a coaching style relationship to enhance student learning" (Barkley, 2011, p. 79). Additional research defines coaching as one-on-one contact focused on the development of students' engagement, academic success, study skills, goal setting, and overall strengths (Robinson & Gahagan, 2010). Though the practice of coaching shares some similarities with other student success strategies, of particular importance is the proactive approach coaches take. It involves both verbal and nonverbal feedback and emphasizes social and behavioral changes for the student being coached (Stormont et al., 2015).

In general, coaching is an approach that can be categorized as a personalized support strategy, which recent research has indicated can help overcome gaps in students' knowledge about what it takes to be successful in college (Bettinger et al., 2009). Personal support has also been found to encourage students to complete critical tasks they might not otherwise complete

(Goldrick-Rab, 2010). The role of a coach has been characterized as helping students establish quantifiable goals and learning activities and skills that will help them be more successful (Martinek, 2006). Using continuous feedback, peer coaches encourage students to reflect on how their behavior shapes their academic success (Robinson & Gahagan, 2010; Truijen & Von Woerkom 2008).

Approaches to coaching identified in the literature vary, though they tend to focus on providing students with opportunities to build academic skills and connecting students to resources. Generally, coaches work to develop a rapport with the student on mutual commonalities to create buy-in to the coaching process, and listen and communicate effectively to motivate the student (Tofade, 2010). Coaching can emphasize different skills and supports for students, including variations on self-assessment, reflection, and goal setting (Grant, 2011; Robinson & Gahagan, 2010; Tofade, 2010). Self-assessment is often used to begin the coaching relationship and help the student and coach set a baseline for understanding the coaching needs of the student. This process of assessment is used to measure a student's current study habits, level of engagement, and other academic skills and can help speed up the timeframe it takes a coach to get to know a student.

Coaches also support and encourage students to improve their academic skills (Melendez, 2007). Coaching is viewed as an intervention strategy based on a collaborative approach that motivates students to improve their academic outcomes by empowering them to take charge of their learning (Barkley, 2011). Coaching can help students cultivate habits that will benefit them academically, including study and time management skills (Bettinger & Baker, 2013). Students who received coaching experienced improvement in their self-regulation and other skills related to academic performance (Bonner, 2010). Some researchers advocated specific areas of focus as part of coaching, including helping a student develop academic skills, problem-solving, and building knowledge (Purwa Udiutoma et al., 2015). By emphasizing problem-solving, coaching can increase the likelihood that students will get more involved in the learning process (Powell & Kalina, 2009). Students who receive coaching have been found to have more developed reflection and collaboration skills, which contributes to increased academic performance (Melendez, 2007).

Coaching can also help acclimate students to life in college. For example, peer coaches can help first-year students adjust to the new expectations that come with transitioning to college. For students who may be unfamiliar with behaviors that promote success in college, coaches can help with improving study skills, connecting with faculty, understanding the learning environment, and being involved on campus (Alkadounmee, 2012). By asking students a variety of open-ended questions to stimulate conversations that may not happen elsewhere on campus, coaches encourage self-reflection. Examples of questions include: "What has been the most positive experience you've had as a college student?" and "Tell me about a time when you enjoyed doing a class project or assignment. What made you feel engaged in this setting?" (Robinson & Gahagan, 2010, p. 28). Self-reflection can encourage students to move away from focusing on the challenge or problem they are facing to identifying and using their resources to find solutions (Grant, 2011). Coaches encourage self-reflection by asking probing, open-ended questions that lead to reflective thought and building their self-awareness and confidence by careful listening and reminding the student of their successes (Tofade, 2010).

Coaching is being utilized in a variety of ways within the higher education context. Researchers have studied coaching as an intervention that can be targeted for specific students, including those struggling academically (Dilmore et al., 2010). Others encourage coaching for all students as a means of achieving personal and academic goals. Though coaching can be offered as a standalone service, coaching can be integrated as part of curriculum-related services and used with individual students or with an entire class to enhance academic performance (Barkley, 2011). Research has found coaching to be particularly useful for first-generation students to help them become familiar with the customs of college life (Hu & Ma, 2010). Now that coaching within the higher education context has been examined, we will highlight a case study where coaching has been implemented in a large public four-year institution.

A Case Study: The First-Year Success Center at Arizona State University

The First-Year Success (FYS) Center at Arizona State University (ASU) provides holistic peer coaching services to over 10,000 first-year students, sophomores, and new transfer students on four university campuses. The FYS Center employs 87 peer success coaches and 11 full-time professional staff. Success coaches are organized into teams based on the student populations they support, and each team is led by a full-time professional senior coordinator or assistant director. The senior coordinator role has three major responsibilities: leading their assigned team of success coaches, serving as liaison between the center and student retention partners, and collaborating on center initiatives, programs, and projects.

The peer success coach position is a complex, multifaceted, and demanding paraprofessional role with a high degree of responsibility. Half of the role is direct student service, and the other half is student outreach and administration. Coaches' work includes conducting coaching appointments; regularly reaching out to their assigned students via phone call, text message, or email; documenting their work with students; and completing reports. One of the ways in which their student employment position is unique is that coaches have access to student information. Coaches are able to view their students' demographic information, contact information, course enrollment, grades, financial aid package, and retention risk indicators. They can also view comments from students' academic advisors and financial aid counselors. Coaches responsibly use this privileged information to provide excellent service to their students. After coaches contact or meet with a student, they input notes from their interactions with that student into a shared data management system, and those comments appear on the student's profile for other student retention and support personnel to be able to view.

The peer success coach position is a highly coveted and highly competitive student employment position. Many applicants indicate they were drawn to the position because they benefited from FYS coaching when they were a first-year student, and they want to have the same positive impact on other students. Coaches are paid a competitive hourly wage, and they work 15 hours per week. To be eligible, students must be a junior or above, and they must have a minimum 3.0 cumulative grade point average. Desired qualifications include student leadership experience, experience working with diverse groups, experience supporting student retention or success, and strong communication skills. The center looks for students who have been successful both inside and outside the classroom. Many selected candidates have prior experience as first-year seminar instructors, residence hall assistants, student organization leaders, mentors, tutors, teaching assistants, college ambassadors, and new student orientation leaders. Others have experience with undergraduate research, internships, community service, or study abroad. Candidates go through a rigorous interview process.

FYS Center professional staff make intentional efforts to recruit a diverse pool of students to apply for the position each year. The goal is to ultimately hire a cohort of coaches whose diversity closely resembles the demographics of the students they will be serving. This diversity is important to the center because it increases the likelihood that students will be able to relate to their coaches. As part of the center's recruitment efforts, emails are sent to eligible candidates, current coaches help with encouraging their friends to apply, and recommendations are sought from student retention and support partners throughout the university.

The success coach training is in alignment with International Coach Federation (ICF) standards. During their initial intensive training before the start of the academic year, coaches learn ICF core competencies such as coaching standards, establishing the coaching agreement, active listening, powerful questioning, and goal setting. Coaches also learn about positive psychology, college student retention, diverse student populations, customer service, empathy, university resources, protocols for working with students of concern, student outreach, technology platforms, self-management, and departmental policies and procedures. Additionally, coaches complete training modules on workplace behavior, the Family Educational Rights and Privacy Act, and information security.

The FYS Center targets over 10,000 students for peer success coaching each year. The target group includes all first-time, full-time, first-year students attending classes on campus with the exception of a few populations who already have specialized support services dedicated to them at the university such as student-athletes, military veterans, and honors students. The target group also includes second-year students whose cumulative grade point average entering their second year is under 3.0. First-year transfer students receive open invitations to participate in peer success coaching, and they are assigned a transfer student success coach upon request.

Target students are automatically matched with a peer success coach based on shared academic campus and college. For example, a student in the business college would be matched with a business college coach. The purpose of matching students based on shared campus and college is for students to be able to meet with a coach who has been successful in that college, understands the resources available within that college, and has similar academic or future career interests.

Each success coach has a portfolio of approximately 130 students that they are tasked with supporting for the entire academic year. To best serve a highly diverse student population, success coaching is customized to each student. Students are able to choose their campus, coaching modality (in person or via phone or Zoom video), frequency of sessions, and topics. Coaching appointments are only 30 minutes, and the center provides a 12-hour service window from Mondays through Thursdays and a 9-hour service window on Fridays to be as accessible as possible to students with varying schedules. As it is a holistic coaching model, students are able to be coached on a variety of topics such as academics, belonging, engagement, mindset, happiness, jobs, internships, research opportunities, navigating the university, personal topics, resilience, scholarships, strengths, and wellness. The success coaching approach draws upon research from higher education retention and positive psychology.

Data consistently show the success of peer success coaching at ASU. The center averages over 15,000 conducted coaching sessions per year, and over 5,200 students participate in coaching each year. The percentage point difference in retention from first year to second year between students who participate in coaching and those who do not participate is 8 to 10 points each year, with larger differences observed for first-generation students and racial and ethnic minorities. Moreover, there is a positive relationship between the number of coaching sessions a student attends and their retention. Student feedback is also overwhelmingly positive, with 98% to 99% of coached students indicating their coach helped them achieve their goals. In surveys, coached students often rave about how much they love coaching and how it has had a positive impact on them. A recent qualitative study focused on the FYS Center highlighted three key findings related to coaching and students receiving coaching (Symonds, 2020).

First, students reported feelings of relatability toward their peer coaches. Students indicated they felt more comfortable discussing their concerns with their coach as compared to other staff or faculty members. Coaching creates an opportunity for coaches to share insider knowledge of campus resources with students from a peer-to-peer perspective. Connecting with a coach who recently experienced what it was like to transition to college and had to learn how to navigate their first semester gave students a sense of comfort. They reported being willing to engage in coaching and discuss more sensitive matters (e.g., difficulty with transition, finding their new friend group, relationship issues), which some students shared they would only discuss with their coach. Also, students felt less intimidated connecting with a peer as compared to faculty and staff. This initial positive experience led students to feel like they could come back and talk to their coach "about anything."

Second, students indicated that peer coaching helped them feel a sense of belonging. Students talked about how important it was for them to connect with their coach, especially until they found their "friend group." As students felt more comfortable with their navigational skills as a result of coaching, they reported embracing their sense of belonging within their campus community. By helping students get more involved, deepen their connection to campus, and feel as though they are cared for, coaching helps students develop a stronger sense of belonging. Given that lack of belonging is one reason that influences students to leave (Tinto, 2001) and that a supportive college environment helps students feel like they fit in (Schwartzman & Sanchez, 2016), it is not surprising that cultivating a sense of belonging was important to both students and coaches.

Finally, students reported that coaching helped them build their self-confidence as college students. As they navigate through the hidden curriculum and other challenges during their transition to college, first-year and first-generation students may suffer decreased self-confidence ("Defining First-Generation," 2017). Lower rates of self-confidence can lead some students to avoid reaching out for help (Longwell-Grice & Longwell-Grice, 2008). Coaches helped increase self-confidence by reinforcing students' pre-existing knowledge, taking a strengths-based approach, celebrating their victories, and helping students feel valued. Though first-generation students are often characterized by the gaps in their knowledge and experience (Harper, 2010; Irizarry, 2009), several coaches shared that students often came to their coaching sessions already armed with the answers they needed. Rather than providing answers to questions or issues students raised, coaching often affirmed students' pre-existing knowledge.

Conclusion

By putting college student retention literature into action, the FYS Center at ASU has achieved remarkable results in college student retention and success. The utilization of peers, holistic and personalized coaching, a strengths-based approach, commitment to serving a diverse student population, extensive training and development, and proactive and ongoing outreach to students have all been essential to the center's success at serving students at scale. The following guiding questions are offered to help colleagues consider how they might increase student retention and success at their own institutions.

Guiding Questions

1. What are the student retention needs at my institution? Do they differ by college, program, or population?
2. What are my institution's strengths with regard to student support and service?
3. What are the institutional barriers to success?
4. Thinking about precollege programs, new student orientation programs, first-year experience, college navigation support, academic progress, and newer developments, how would we like to focus our time, energy, and resources?

References

Alkadounmee, K. (2012). The effect of a training program for developing the social skills in reducing the chaotic behavior of at-risk students of academic failure. *European Journal of Social Sciences, 29*, 537–552.

Barkley, A. (2011). Academic coaching for enhanced learning. *NACTA Journal, 51*(1), 76–81.

Bean, J. P., & Metzner, B. S. (1985). A conceptual model of nontraditional undergraduate student attrition. *Review of Educational Research, 55*(4), 485–540.

Bettinger, E., & Baker, R. (2011). *The effects of student coaching in college: An evaluation of a randomized experiment in student mentoring* (NBER No. w16881). National Bureau of Economic Research.

Bettinger, E. P., Long, B. T., Oreopoulos, P., & Sanbonmatsu, L. (2009). *The role of simplification and information in college decisions: Results from the H&R Block FAFSA Experiment* (NBER Working Paper No. 15361). National Bureau of Economic Research.

Bonner, J. (2010). Taking a stand as a student-centered research university: Active and collaborative learning meets scholarship of teaching at the University of Alabama. *Journal of General Education, 59*, 183–192. doi:10.1353/jge.2010.0022

Bransberger, P., & Michelau, D. K. (2016). *Knocking at the college door: Projections of high school graduates*. Western Interstate Commission for Higher Education.

Braxton, J. M., Brier, E. M., & Steele, S. L. (2007). Shaping retention from research to practice. *Journal of College Student Retention: Research, Theory & Practice, 9*, 377–399.

Campbell, T. A., & Campbell, D. E. (1997). Faculty/student mentor program: Effects on academic performance and retention. *Research in Higher Education, 38*, 727–742.

Cardoza, K. (2016). First-generation college students are not succeeding in college, and money isn't the problem. *The Washington Post*, 1, 20.

Cataldi, E. F., Bennett, C. T., Chen, X., & Simone, S. A. (2018). *First-generation students: College access, persistence, and postbachelor's outcomes*. National Center for Education Statistics.

Conley, D. T. (2007). Toward a more comprehensive conception of college readiness. Educational Policy Improvement Center. https://docs.gatesfoundation.org/documents/collegereadinesspaper.pdf

Correa, K. (2017). *Retaining out-of-state freshmen at ASU* (Publication No. 10271169) [Doctoral dissertation, Arizona State University]. ProQuest Dissertations and Theses Global.

Crisp, G., & Cruz, I. (2009). Mentoring college students: A critical review of the literature between 1990 and 2007. *Research in Higher Education, 50*(6), 525–545.

Defining first-generation. (2017, November 20). Center for First-Generation Success. https://firstgen.naspa.org/blog/defining-first-generation

Dilmore, T. C., Rubio, D. M., Cohen, E., Seltzer, D., Switzer, G. E., Bryce, C., & Kapoor, W. N. (2010). Psychometric properties of the mentor role instrument when used in an academic medicine setting. *Clinical and Translational Science, 3*, 104–108. doi:10.1111/j.1752-8062.2010.00196.x

Drake, J. K., Jordan, P., & Miller, M. A. (Eds.). (2013). *Academic advising approaches: Strategies that teach students to make the most of college*. Jossey-Bass.

Education Advisory Board. (2016). Persistence rates rise, especially for some nontraditional students. https://www.eab.com/daily-briefing/2016/05/11/persistence-rates-rise-especially-for-some-nontraditional-students

Engle, J., & O'Brien, C. (2007). *Demography is not destiny: Increasing the graduation rates of low-income college students at large public universities*. Pell Institute for the Study of Opportunity in Higher Education.

Engle, J., & Tinto, V. (2008). *Moving beyond access: College success for low-income, first- generation students*. Pell Institute for the Study of Opportunity in Higher Education.

Gershenfeld, S. (2014). A review of undergraduate mentoring programs. *Review of Educational Research, 84*, 365–391.

Girves, J. E., Zepeda, Y., & Gwathmey, J. K. (2005). Mentoring in a post-affirmative action world. *Journal of Social Issues, 61*, 449–479.

Goldrick-Rab, S. (2010). Challenges and opportunities for improving community college student success. *Review of Educational Research, 80*, 437–469.

Grant, A. M. (2011). The Solution-Focused Inventory—A tripartite taxonomy for teaching, measuring and conceptualizing solution-focused approaches to coaching. *Coaching Psychologist, 7*, 98–106.

Hagedorn, L. S., Maxwell, W., Rodriguez, P., Hocevar, D., & Fillpot, J. (2000). Peer and student-faculty relations in community colleges. *Community College Journal of Research & Practice, 24*, 587–598.

Harper, S. R. (2010). An anti-deficit achievement framework for research on students of color in STEM. *New Directions for Institutional Research, 2010*(148), 63–74.

Hayes, D. (2012). A winning strategy. *Diverse: Issues in Higher Education, 29*(16), 14–15.

Hu, S., & Ma, Y. (2010). Mentoring and student persistence in college: A study of the Washington State Achievers Program. *Innovative Higher Education, 35*(5), 329–341.

Hurtado, S., & Carter, D. F. (1997). Effects of college transition and perceptions of the campus racial climate on Latino college students' sense of belonging. *Sociology of Education, 70*(4), 324–345.

Irizarry, J. (2009). *Characteristics of the cultural deficit model.* Gale Cengage Learning: Education.com.

Ishiyama, J. (2007). Expectations and perceptions of undergraduate research mentoring: Comparing first-generation, low income white/Caucasian and African American students. *College Student Journal, 41*(3), 540.

Jaasma, M. A., & Koper, R. J. (1999). The relationship of student-faculty out-of-class communication to instructor immediacy and trust and to student motivation. *Communication Education, 48*, 41–47.

Kim, Y. K., & Sax, L. J. (2009). Student–faculty interaction in research universities: Differences by student gender, race, social class, and first-generation status. *Research in Higher Education, 50*, 437–459.

Kuh, G., Kinzie, J., Buckley, J., Bridges, B., & Hayek, J. (2006). What matters to student success: A review of the literature spearheading a dialog on student success. *Commissioned Report for the National Symposium on Postsecondary Student Success Spearheading a Dialog on Student Success, 18*(July), 156. https://nces.ed.gov/npec/pdf/Kuh_Team_Report.pdf

Latino, J. A., & Unite, C. M. (2012). Providing academic support through peer education. *New Directions for Higher Education, 157*, 31–43. doi:10.1002/he.20004

Light, R. J. (2004). *Making the most of college: Students speak their minds.* Harvard University Press.

Longwell-Grice, R., & Longwell-Grice, H. (2007). Testing Tinto: How do retention theories work for first-generation, working-class students? *Journal of College Student Retention: Research, Theory and Practice, 9*, 407–420. doi:10.2190/CS.9.4.a

Luna, G., & Cullen, D. L. (1995). *Empowering the faculty: Mentoring redirected and renewed.* ERIC Digest.

Malm, M., Madsen, L. M., & Lundmark, A. M. (2020). Students' negotiations of belonging in geoscience: Experiences of faculty-student interactions when entering university. *Journal of Geography in Higher Education, 44*(4), 532–549. https://doi.org/10.1080/03098265.2020.1771683

Mangold, W. D., Bean, L. G., Adams, D. J., Schwab, W. A., & Lynch, S. M. (2003). Who goes who stays: An assessment of the effect of a freshman mentoring and unit registration program on college persistence. *Journal of College Student Retention, 4*(2), 95–122.

Martinek, G. (2006). Coaching positive behavior support in school settings tactics and data- based decision making. *Journal of Positive Behavior Interventions, V*(I), 165–173. doi:10.1177/10983007060080030501

Melendez, R. (2007). Coaching students to achieve their goals: Can it boost retention. *Hispanic Outlook in Higher Education, 17*, 21–60.

Milem, J. F., & Berger, J. B. (1997). A modified model of college student persistence: Exploring the relationship between Astin's theory of involvement and Tinto's theory of student departure. *Journal of College Student Development, 38*(4), 387–400.

Mu, L., & Fosnacht, K. (2019). Effective advising: How academic advising influences student learning outcomes in different institutional contexts. *Review of Higher Education, 42*(4), 1283–1307. https://doi.org/10.1353/rhe.2019.0066

Muraskin, L. (1997). "Best practices" in student support services: A study of five exemplary sites. http://www2.ed.gov/offices/OUS/PES/higher/5study.pdf

Pagan, R., & Edwards-Wilson, R. (2003). A mentoring program for remedial students. *Journal of College Student Retention, 4*, 207–225.

Pascarella, E. T., Terenzini, P. T., & Blimling, G. S. (1994). The impact of residential life on students. In C. C. Schroeder & P. Mable (Eds.), *Realizing the educational potential of residence halls* (pp. 22–52). University of Michigan.

Pike, G. R., & Kuh, G. D. (2005). First-and second-generation college students: A comparison of their engagement and intellectual development. *Journal of Higher Education, 76*(3), 276–300.

Powell, K. C., & Kalina, C. J. (2009). Cognitive and social constructivism: Developing tools for an effective classroom. *Education, 130*(2), 241–250.

Purwa Udiutoma, S. T., Srinovita, Y., & Si, S. (2015). The effect of coaching and mentoring programs to improve students' competencies: A case study of Beastudi Etos scholarship. *Universal Journal of Educational Research, 3*, 163–169. doi:10.13189/ujer2015.030302

Robinson, C., & Gahagan, J. (2010). Coaching students to academic success and engagement on campus. *About Campus, 15*(4), 26–29.

Salinitri, G. (2005). The effects of formal mentoring on the retention rates for first-year, low-achieving students. *Canadian Journal of Education, 28*, 853–873.

Schwartzman, R., & Sanchez, R. (2016). Communication centers as sites for identity (re) negotiation. *College Student Journal, 50*, 35–46.

Smith, B. (2009). *Mentoring programs: The great hope or great hype?* Critical Essay. ASHE/Lumina Fellows Series, Issue 7. Association for the Study of Higher Education.

Stormont, M., Reinke, W. M., Newcomer, L., Marchese, D., & Lewis, C. (2015). Coaching teachers' use of social behavior interventions to improve children's outcomes: A review of the literature. *Journal of Positive Behavior Interventions, 17*, 69–82.

Symonds, S. (2020). *Been there, done that: Peer coaching and community cultural wealth* (Publication No. 28029320) [Doctoral dissertation, Arizona State University]. ProQuest Dissertations and Theses Global.

Tinto, V. (1993). *Leaving college: Rethinking the causes and cures of student attrition* (2nd ed.). University of Chicago Press.

Tinto, V. (1999). Taking retention seriously: Rethinking the first year of college. *NACADA Journal, 19*, 5–9.

Tinto, V. (2001). *Rethinking the first year of college.* Higher Education Monograph Series, Syracuse University.

Tinto, V. (2008, June 9). Access without support is not opportunity. *Inside Higher Ed.* https://www.insidehighered.com/views/2008/06/09/access-without-support-not-opportunity

Tofade, T. (2010). Coaching younger practitioners and students using components of the co-active coaching model. *American Journal of Pharmaceutical Education, 74*(3), 1–5.

Torres, V., & Hernandez, E. (2009). Influence of an identified advisor/mentor on urban Latino students' college experience. *Journal of College Student Retention: Research, Theory & Practice, 11*, 141–160.

Truijen, K. J., & Van Woerkom, M. (2008). The pitfalls of collegial coaching: An analysis of collegial coaching in medical education and its influence on stimulating reflection and performance of novice clinical teachers. *Journal of Workplace Learning, 20*, 316–326.

White, E., & Schulenberg, J. (2012). Academic advising—A focus on learning. *About Campus, 16*(6), 11–17.

Zalaquett, C. P., & Lopez, A. D. (2006). Learning from the stories of successful undergraduate Latina/Latino students: The importance of mentoring. *Mentoring & Tutoring, 14*, 337–353.

Zinshteyn, M. (2016). The stress of paying for college. *The Atlantic*. https://www.theatlantic.com/education/archive/2016/02/the-widespread-stress-over-paying-for-college/462984/

8

"Guiding My Success"

Providing a Developmental Lens to Strengthen the Whole Person

Larry J. Nelson

As editor of the Oxford Series on Emerging Adulthood, I am extremely excited about the contribution this book is going to make to the series. It seems there is a growing disconnect between those who study the development of emerging adults and those who work with them in the context of higher education. For example, for years, there has been a charge to those of us who study emerging adults to expand beyond samples drawn from college students. In fact, several journals have taken rather strong stances against publishing articles that employ samples that include only students. Much of this push to move beyond college student samples has been made with good intentions in hopes to better understand development in a broader range of the emerging adult population. However, in doing so, it fails to recognize the large number of emerging adults who might be served by understanding the role of development in their pursuit of higher education. Conversely, when in my current role as president of the Society for the Study of Emerging Adulthood I examine the professional positions of our members and those who attend our professional meetings, I seldom see listed among them individuals in administrative positions at institutions of higher education. I think there will be negative consequences if we continue to see the gap widen between those who study and work with emerging adults in higher education specifically and those who study emerging adult development. As a result, I cannot underscore enough how important I feel this book is in bringing a developmental lens to promoting student success in higher education.

I have recently had a front-row seat to what can happen when we separate the development of emerging adults from the context of higher education. At about the same time that I was asked to write this chapter, I was also assigned to serve on a committee at my institution to redesign our General Education program. Little did I know at the time how much the

Larry J. Nelson, *"Guiding My Success"* In: *Cultivating Student Success.* Edited by: Tisha A. Duncan and Allison A. Buskirk-Cohen, Oxford University Press. © Oxford University Press 2022. DOI: 10.1093/oso/9780197586693.003.0009 experience of sitting on that committee would underscore the need for this book, generally, and for what I hope to contribute in this chapter, specifically. "Flourishing" from the perspective of positive psychology has been described as high levels of emotional, psychological, and social well-being that lead to productive engagement with others and in society (Keyes & Haidt, 2003). When looked at specifically as it applies to student success and persistence, the term "thriving" has been conceptualized to include academic engagement and performance, interpersonal relationships, and psychological well-being (Schreiner et al., 2012). Many of the members of our faculty serving on this committee could readily see the need for academic engagement and performance and, as a result, could easily list the skills that they wanted students to develop in this area to succeed. However, repeatedly, many of my colleagues (faculty and administrators) either could not grasp what a holistic, or whole-person, view of student development even included (despite repeated attempts to explain) or overtly dismissed the need for any such approach within an academic setting. It has been incredibly frustrating to listen to well-intentioned people discuss student thriving but do so with total disregard for the role that interpersonal competence and psychological well-being play in the process.

I have wondered if the inability to see the need for a holistic approach as essential for student success speaks to why we are not meeting the needs of our students (whether assessed via declining enrollment, retention rates, etc.). In other words, if instructors believe that the role of higher education is to focus solely on conveying academic information, they are ignoring the evidence that students flourish when they develop the entire person (e.g., Schreiner et al., 2009). It is wrong to think that academic engagement can be separated from interpersonal and intrapersonal well-being. Indeed, we need to see and understand that all of these areas are interconnected (Schreiner, 2012) and situated within the context of where emerging adults are in the development.

In the end, I think some of the challenges of getting some people to see student success through the lens of the whole person may reside in a lack of understanding of human development and the role it plays in flourishing and floundering, generally, and student success, specifically. In its simplest definition, human development is the study of how people grow, change, and stay the same throughout their lives (Kuther, 2019). Development throughout one's life occurs in various dimensions including physical, cognitive, and socioemotional domains. These domains are interdependent as change or stability in one area is related to change or stability in another. For example, academic performance is not just affected by one's cognitive development but also by one's physical (hungry or sick), social (e.g., being bullied), or emotional (e.g., anxiety, depression) state. As such, development is affected by many aspects of one's physical body (e.g., brain growth, genetics, hormones, autonomic nervous system), as well as the numerous contexts within which a person resides (e.g., peer groups, families, campus, culture).

Based on this brief summary of development, I think a lack of understanding of development is problematic because many faculty and institutional administrators may think that academic success can be separated from development. Specifically, it is naïvely optimistic to think that we can effectively educate students in academic skills (e.g., critical thinking, writing) and disciplinary knowledge without consideration of the whole person's development (i.e., brain development, the interrelatedness of various aspects of their lives, etc.). Admittedly, some people within our institutions may recognize the importance of addressing various aspects of development, but again, they often try to compartmentalize the domains of development to various places on our campuses. For example, in working on this committee, I have heard repeatedly that we do not need to build a view of the whole person into a general education program because there are already counseling and advisement centers on campus for those who are struggling. Such a view fails to recognize that the absence of "negative" does not mean the presence of "positive." In other words, the attempts to *remediate* indices of maladjustment or risk (i.e., anxiety, depression, poor study skills, etc.) is not the same as *promoting* indices of cognitive, physical, and socioemotional adjustment and competence. Furthermore, a view that focuses mainly on those few who might be most at risk of negative outcomes (while absolutely *essential* to do) ignores the need for an institutional approach to fostering success and well-being of the entire student body.

The call for a holistic approach to foster student success and engagement is not new (see Schreiner et al., 2012). However, it is exciting to be part of a book that meets students where they are—emotionally, in their pursuit of identity, living in a media-saturated world—in the attempt to promote success in higher education. The contribution that I hope to make in this chapter is to provide a broad developmental lens to the discussion. Specifically, the purpose of this chapter is to examine emerging adulthood (ages 18 to 29) as the developmental context for fostering students' academic success, interpersonal relationships, and psychological well-being while pursuing their education and to better situate them for flourishing thereafter as members of society.

Developmental Deficiencies: The Need to Focus on the Whole Person

As noted, the traditional college student is in a period of life that is now commonly referred to as emerging adulthood (ages 18 to 29). Despite age 18 being designated as the legal age of adulthood in the United States, we now know that most young people attending college do not consider themselves to be adults (nor do their parents; Nelson et al., 2007). Furthermore, everything that we know about development shows that growth in a variety of domains continues to occur after the age of 18. Thus, we need to examine emerging adulthood as the developmental context in which higher education resides. In other words, the development of individuals does not occur because of colleges and universities, but rather, just as children attend elementary school and teenagers attend high school, institutions of higher education are a context in which developing emerging adults place themselves. Therefore, just as the approach to education in elementary school and high school, respectively, is targeted to where young people are in their development, we likewise need to understand development to effectively educate the whole person in higher education.

One of the most important aspects to understand about development in emerging adulthood is that it is a unique period in brain development. It was previously thought that brain development was finished by the end of adolescence. We now know that changes in the brain (i.e., synaptic pruning, myelination of the prefrontal cortex, and changes in the limbic system) begin in early adolescence but do not end with a fully developed brain until well into the 20s (Steinberg, 2008; Taber-Thomas & Perez-Edgar, 2016). Until the brain is fully developed, young people still struggle with the ability to calculate risk, delay gratification, think rationally and beyond the moment, and control emotions. Furthermore, they tend to be easily distracted, often overgeneralize, and powerfully experience emotion, passion, and pleasure (see Steinberg, 2008; Taber-Thomas & Perez-Edgar, 2016).

Why does understanding brain development matter for today's colleges and universities more than in the past? Throughout childhood and adolescence, youth experience a great deal of structure as they are under the protective care of parents, daycare providers, teachers, and other adults (e.g., coaches, employers) throughout much (if not all) of the day. Within this structure, boundaries are provided in that adults say when things should occur (e.g., bedtime), provide rules for what behavior is expected (e.g., in the classroom), and mete out consequences for when those expectations are not met. This structure is necessary because children do not yet have the cognitive, linguistic, social, or emotional maturity (i.e., competence) to exercise complete autonomy. Compared to children, adolescents are given greater (but not complete) autonomy to make choices because, on average, competence in these areas (i.e., cognitive, social, emotional, etc.) is growing.

Upon entering emerging adulthood, young people are granted even more autonomy in the belief that competence in these areas has grown. Unfortunately, the incorrect perception has evolved over time that brain development is complete and cognitive, linguistic, social, and emotional competence has been achieved by the age of 18. In fact, neither brain development nor competence in these areas has been achieved by age 18, but now young people are given almost complete autonomy to decide how to spend their time and who to spend it with. As such, we tend to give more autonomy to young people who have (1) very little structure, (2) brains that are still developing, and (3) levels of competence (emotional, cognitive, social, etc.) that are not yet mature. With such a combination, it is not surprising that emerging adulthood is a period in which many young people are floundering (Nelson & Padilla-Walker, 2013). Specifically, this may explain why the 20s have become the peak period in the life course for alcohol and drug use (Andrews & Westling, 2016), driving while drunk (Centers for Disease Control and Prevention, 2019), risky sexual practices (Lam & Lefkowitz, 2013), and reckless behaviors that are potentially life threatening to oneself or others (see Park et al., 2014). Furthermore, it is the period of time with the highest risk of being a victim of a violent crime (e.g., U.S. Department of Justice, 2019), as well as the decade with the highest rates of perpetuating a crime (see Craig & Piquero, 2016). Also, the instability felt by many young people (Nelson et al., 2015) due to the lack of structure may account for why it is a period with high rates of self-harm, disordered eating, anxiety, depression, and challenges in many other aspects of mental health (World Health Organization, 2016). Taken together, these externalizing and internalizing challenges may explain why the leading causes of death in industrialized nations between ages 18 and 30 are accidents and suicide (e.g., World Health Organization, 2016).

The question may be asked, what does any of this have to do with institutions of higher learning? In the past, earlier entry into contexts such as full-time careers (that did not require higher education), marriage, and the military provided a level of structure for young people as their brain developed and their socioemotional competence continued to grow. Lacking (on average) those or any other forms of institutional structure, colleges and universities remain as one of the few large-scale forms of organizational structure for many emerging adults. To dismiss that fact, or to attempt to deny responsibility for providing structure, is to naïvely ignore the reality of where our students are in their development (underdeveloped brain, not yet competent in domains of development, etc.). In doing so, we will continue to watch enrollment rates drop, retention rates decline, and floundering increase as young people's developmental needs are not met and the deficiencies of development overwhelm them. Again, "optimal functioning in three key areas that contribute to student success and persistence" include academic engagement and performance, interpersonal relationships, and psychological well-being (Schreiner, 2012, p. 4). In understanding development and, therefore, taking a holistic approach to educating students, universities can provide structure within which this optimal functioning can be achieved.

The effects of COVID-19 on higher education and its students can provide an example of just how important the role of structure is in fostering student success. Because of the size of my enrollments, I now offer my introduction to human development course "on demand," meaning that I post lectures for students to watch on their own. I have also created videos on how to write their papers and how to study for my exams. In an attempt to provide some structure, I provided a syllabus with a daily schedule of when they should watch certain lectures and complete assignments, and I assigned due dates along the way to keep them on pace to complete the course by the end of the semester. Despite my efforts to provide them with structure, without a built-in time for lectures, some students are falling behind. Many adults might mistakenly attribute this to a growing deficiency in young people to be responsible when, instead, it reflects the developmental need for some structure during a time that is otherwise lacking it and during a developmental period when the underdeveloped brain leaves young people vulnerable in areas of distractibility, delay of gratification, and thinking rationally and beyond the moment (see Steinberg, 2008; Taber-Thomas & Perez-Edgar, 2016).

Higher education must recognize where young people are in development and (1) accept its role in providing the structure that will facilitate learning and (2) attend to the developmental needs of the whole person in ways that will foster success. Without this holistic approach and structure, the developmental challenges of the time period will continue to place young people at risk for floundering. For example, in a study of college students from around the United States, my colleague and I identified a group of college students who were flourishing and two groups of students (composed mostly of men) who were floundering (Nelson & Padilla-Walker, 2013). One group that was floundering exhibited very high levels of externalizing problems such as binge drinking, drug use, risky sexual behaviors, and heavy violent video game use. Another group exhibited a lot of these same behaviors but also struggled with some problems of an internalizing nature such as low self-esteem and depressive symptoms. The deficiencies of an underdeveloped brain are evident in these findings (i.e., lower ability to calculate risk, delay gratification, think rationally and beyond the moment, and control emotions), but so too are the deficiencies in interpersonal and psychological competencies. And this is the important point, the lack of interpersonal and intrapersonal competence exhibited in these floundering groups are the same skills lacking in many students who struggle in their academic pursuits. There is not much that can be done to expedite brain growth as it is simply a function of individual maturational timing, but to the extent that brain growth will allow, intrapersonal and interpersonal skills can be taught to foster competence in areas such as self-control, emotion regulation, prioritizing, consequential thinking, time management, internal motivations, perspective taking, and so many more.

As such, an institutional focus on the whole person can decrease indices of floundering and, simultaneously, increase academic performance and campus engagement because it builds on where young people are developmentally. How does a student build relationships (e.g., an integral indicator of student engagement and success; Nelson & Vetter, 2012) or work in groups in the classroom without communication and other social skills? How do we expect students to have the self-control to focus on course assignments when they do not have the self-control to turn off forms of media (e.g., video games)? Do we have realistic expectations that our students can engage in meaningful learning strategies that include trial and error without helping them to learn to cope with perfectionism or examining their learning motivations (i.e., external vs. internal)? Do institutions of higher education incorrectly assume that in turning 18 all of the intrapersonal and interpersonal competencies are fully developed and only academic development is needed? Or, similarly, do we hope that the development of interpersonal and intrapersonal competence will just naturally occur somehow as we focus on academic engagement within disciplinary curriculum? Or, conversely, do we recognize that, developmentally, (1) young people are not yet competent in these key areas of development and (2) these competencies are absolutely requisite for academic success? If we acknowledge the latter, then, as a result, we can take an explicit and direct approach to addressing the developmental needs of the whole person that will, in turn, contribute to academic success and engagement. In sum, only in understanding where young people are in their development can we begin to think about a holistic approach to higher education.

Leveraging Development

Thus far in this chapter I have given most of the attention to developmental deficiencies. I would like to now focus on some of the aspects of what emerging adults are experiencing developmentally that can be seen as adaptive and potentially beneficial in how we think about helping students thrive. In his theory of emerging adulthood, Arnett (2000, 2015) proposes that there are distinct features of this time period that set it apart as a unique period of development in the life course, including *identity exploration* (especially in the areas of work, love, and worldviews), *instability* (seen in changes of direction in residential status, relationships, work, and education), *focus on the self* (not self-centered but simply lacking obligations to others such as spouse or children), *feeling in-between* (do not see themselves as either adolescents or adults), and *possibilities* (potential to steer their lives in any number of desired directions). By understanding these key features of the time period, it may be possible to leverage them in ways that foster student success and engagement.

For example, one of the central tasks of development in emerging adulthood is identity development. Young people develop their identity, or a coherent sense of self, as they explore, choose, and adhere to a specific set of goals, values, and beliefs (Erikson, 1968). The process of identity formation relates not only to education and career choices but also to one's identity as it relates to love (e.g., sexuality, romantic relationships), values, worldviews (e.g., political perspectives), religious affiliation, gender, and ethnicity (e.g., ethnic identity refers to the extent to which one has considered the subjective importance of one's ethnic or cultural group; see Syed & Mitchell, 2013). As noted previously, although the process of identity development certainly begins in adolescence, we now understand that the process is a central feature of development during emerging adulthood as it is only then that exposure to a greater variety of possibilities, the contexts to explore them, and the autonomy to actively explore in breadth and depth (and then commit to and identify with the choices) fully exist (Arnett, 2015). Thus, for students, college campuses become a rich context for identity formation in nearly all of the areas of identity noted. Hence, again, to try to narrowly define the role of a college or university to assist young people in their educational and career identity naïvely ignores students' developmental interest and drive to use their campus experience to fully and holistically explore themselves. It would be academically arrogant to think that campus services, initiatives, activities, courses, and majors are purely academic undertakings instead of resources used by students to discover a sense of who one is as a whole person as motivated to do so by deep developmental drives to answer the question: who am I?

Thus, colleges and universities should not shy away from attempts to meet students where they are in development (i.e., striving for identity formation). Instead, they should leverage development in all they do so as to, at a minimum, foster interest in enrollment and improve retention, but ultimately to promote student thriving as they nurture academic success and engagement. If students developmentally are engaged in the process of identity exploration and they are explicitly provided opportunities to do that (i.e., as part of their general education courses, campus services and activities, first-year experiences, learning communities, etc.), then their education now becomes personal to them and, therefore, integration, engagement, success, and well-being are likely outcomes. Indeed, having made progress in the identity process (i.e., achievement) is linked to numerous indices of well-being including self-esteem, life satisfaction, better mental health (less anxiety and fewer depressive symptoms), purpose in life, internal locus of control, feeling like an adult, and feeling comfortable in school (Luyckx et al., 2008; Nelson & Barry, 2005; Schwartz, 2007; Schwartz et al., 2009, 2011; Waterman, 2007). In sum, identity development is a key component of emerging adults' development, and rather than ignoring it or dismissing its relevance, institutions can leverage its importance by acknowledging it and facilitating it as a means to enhance students' academic engagement and success.

Although identity development is probably the most central feature of emerging adulthood, there are certainly other aspects that might be leveraged to foster student success and engagement. In particular, emerging adulthood is an age of possibilities and optimism in which young people have high hopes and great expectations for their future (Arnett, 2015). Anybody who has worked with college students has experienced their idealistic vision of wanting to change the world. Oftentimes, indecision regarding a major is not because they do not know what to do but rather because they want to do it all! And not only do they want to change the world, but also they want to start changing it *right now*. Oftentimes these motivated and energetic students feel held back by any hoop to jump through (e.g., any class that does not seem to be connected to their vision of changing the world) because they want to get started on creating the world they want to live in. This is not a bad thing but simply an incredible force that needs to be given direction. Do our current structures (e.g., general education) douse that flame or fan it? Does understanding this key aspect of the development of emerging adults help us understand why service learning has been promoted as a key strategy for fostering student involvement during a first-year experience aimed at promoting student engagement and retention (Nelson & Vetter, 2012)? How else can this developmental idealism be leveraged to facilitate student success?

Emerging adulthood as an age of possibilities and optimism does not just refer to young people's desire to change the world. It also refers to the potential to dramatically change the direction of their own lives. Arnett (2015) notes that it is difficult for children and adolescents to rise above a chaotic or unhappy family life because they reside in that environment every day. Emerging adulthood then becomes the time to "straighten the parts of themselves that have become twisted" (Arnett, 2015, p. 16). Even for those who come from rather well-adjusted family circumstances, emerging adulthood is an opportunity to become the person they desire to be in *all domains of their lives.* While many universities and critics of higher education may see academic/career development as the sole purpose of higher education, young people cannot and do not separate the two. Students are sorting out the challenges brought on by difficult family backgrounds, negative peer group experiences (e.g., bullying), and larger contextual risk factors (e.g., prejudice, poverty, systemic racism) *at the same time* they are trying to succeed in college classes. These personal challenges have the potential to shape the experience students have on our campuses, but fortunately, an intentional approach to addressing the development of the whole person on our campuses can assist young people in their developmental strivings to change and improve their own lives. Any attempt to focus only on a singular aspect of young people's development (i.e., academics) is a naïve and artificial dissecting of the lives of young people who, in their attempt and desire to improve in all areas of their lives, do not set aside all other aspects of their development while attending school. By recognizing that our students desire to develop themselves fully to reach their own potential and to change the world, we can leverage this in all aspects of campus life to assist them in thriving academically, interpersonally, and interpersonally.

This is not intended to be a complete overview of all aspects of development that may be leveraged to foster thriving. Instead, it is meant to provide a few examples of how understanding where students are developmentally might serve to broaden our perspectives of the need to educate the whole student, and how we might leverage development in ways to do that effectively.

Educating with the Long View

To underscore the need to educate the whole person through a developmental lens, I would like to conclude the chapter by taking the long view of the role that higher education can have in the lives of students. My colleagues and I have recently completed a study examining how flourishing and floundering in 30- to 35-year-olds is tied to choices and behaviors experienced in their

20s. The preliminary findings are demonstrating that education is a central factor in well-being in early adulthood (Leonhardt et al., 2019). These early results are showing that getting an education during emerging adulthood is positively associated with not only income (as might be expected) but also a much broader range of indices of well-being including life satisfaction, emotional and physical health, less regret, and feelings of hope in early adulthood (Lott, 2019). Some may argue that these positive findings are all a result of the financial security provided by the higher income of college graduates, but the results emerged after controlling for household income. In other words, gaining an education appears to be associated with individuals' well-being in many domains of their lives.

This may lead many to then claim that the current approach, focusing mainly on the academic domain, is doing just fine. However, these findings underscore the potential that higher education has in benefiting the whole person. In other words, if these moderate correlations can be found in an approach to higher education that often focuses mainly on one domain of development only, it is exciting to consider what could be done to improve well-being in the life trajectories of students coming from institutions that give intentional attention to the developmental needs of emerging adults and, in doing so, attend to the whole person. In an era in which institutions of higher education are under attack by those who judge its worth solely by economic indices (e.g., high costs, excessive dept, whether a major can lead to a specific job), it is important that higher education can demonstrate that a university education compared to education focused solely on a trade has the potential to have long-lasting benefits in the lives of students. These benefits extend far beyond a paycheck but into numerous indices of health and well-being in life, especially if those various domains of the whole person are intentionally attended to as part of the pursuit of higher education.

Conclusion

The purpose of this chapter was to examine emerging adulthood (ages 18 to 29) as the developmental context for fostering students' academic success, interpersonal relationships, and psychological well-being (Schreiner, 2012). In doing this, I noted that many experts in higher education and student affairs, and related disciplines, have done exceptional work showing the need to attend not only to the academic growth of students but also to their interpersonal and intrapersonal competence. Hence, my emphasis on the need to educate the whole person is not new. However, I have attempted to provide the developmental lens of what is occurring during emerging adulthood (e.g., brain development, identity development, lack of structure) that might help frame why a focus on the whole person is indeed so important. Furthermore, in providing this developmental backdrop to students' pursuit of education, I hope to have underscored how a developmental approach to educating the whole person can broaden the aim and scope of campus initiatives, programs, and courses in ways to leverage development in efforts to promote thriving.

Next Steps and Recommendations

Throughout this chapter, I have attempted to outline the need to integrate educating the total person into the aims of higher education by better understanding where our students are developmentally. I have provided some examples throughout, but allow me to close this chapter by providing a few broad recommendations to better achieve what I have called for:

- There should be more dual-track PhD programs in human development and higher education and student affairs. At the very least, programs focusing on higher education specifically should make sure that courses in human development/developmental psychology focused on emerging adulthood should be required.
- Discipline-specific professional organizations should promote attempts to communicate more. For example, professional meetings of organizations focused on higher educations might have special sessions on developmental issues or have invited speakers from developmental organizations speak on important developmental topics related to the particular theme of the meetings. Conversely, developmental organizations such as the Society for the Study of Emerging Adulthood and others might have special sessions and invited speakers with expertise in higher education speak to how the theme of the conference would promote success in higher education.
- This book provides an example of cross-disciplinary collaborations that might close the gap between those working with emerging adults in higher education and those who study factors that lead to flourishing and floundering in emerging adult development generally. More scholarly collaborations such as this are needed in the form of books, special issues in journals, webinars, etc.
- More and better research is needed to identify the outcome of efforts to educate the whole person from a developmental perspective. In fact, it

may be that the best practices of programs (e.g., first-year experience, learning communities) that are successful at fostering student success are doing so because they are (knowingly or not) developing the whole person, which, in turn, is driving the positive academic outcomes. Chapter 7 describes such a program; additional work is needed to evaluate the specific mechanisms that might make this program and others like it effective.

References

Andrews, J. A., & Westling, E. (2016). Substance use in emerging adulthood. In J. J. Arnett (Ed.), *Oxford library of psychology. The Oxford handbook of emerging adulthood* (pp. 521–542). Oxford University Press.

Arnett, J. J. (2000). Emerging adulthood: A theory of development from the late teens through the twenties. *American Psychologist, 55*, 469–480.

Arnett, J. J. (2015). *Emerging adulthood: The winding road from the late teens through the twenties* (2nd ed.). Oxford University Press.

Centers for Disease Control and Prevention. (2019). Impaired driving: Get the facts. https://www.cdc.gov/motorvehiclesafety/impaired_driving/impaired-drv_factsheet.html

Craig, J. M., & Piquero, A. R. (2016). Crime and punishment in emerging adulthood. In J. J Arnett (Ed.), *Handbook of emerging adulthood* (pp. 543–558). Oxford University Press.

Erikson, E. H. (1968). *Identity: Youth and crisis.* Norton & Co.

Keyes, C. L. M., & Haidt, J. (Eds.). (2003). *Flourishing: Positive psychology and the life well-lived.* American Psychological Association. https://doi.org/10.1037/10594-000

Kuther, T. L. (2019). *Lifespan development in context: A topical approach.* Sage.

Lam, C. B., & Lefkowitz, E. S. (2013). Risky sexual behaviors in emerging adults: Longitudinal changes and within-person variations. *Archives of Sexual Behavior, 42*, 523–532. doi:10.1007/s10508-012-9959-x

Leonhardt, N., Nelson, L.J., Willoughby, B., Palmer, C., & Lott, M. (2019). Time of reckoning: Examining the relations between decisions made in emerging adulthood and flourishing or floundering in early adulthood. Paper presented at the biennial meeting of the Society for the Study of Emerging Adulthood, Toronto, Canada, October, 2019.

Lott, M. L. (2019). *Decade of choices: Associations between choices during the twenties and flourishing or floundering during the thirties.* Unpublished thesis.

Luyckx, K., Schwartz, S. J., Goossens, L., & Pollock, S. (2008). Employment, sense of coherence, and identity formation: Contextual and psychological processes on the pathway to sense of adulthood. *Journal of Adolescent Research, 23*, 566–591.

Nelson, D. D., & Vetter, D. (2012). Thriving in the first college year. In L. A. Schreiner, M. C. Laurie, & D. D. Nelson (Eds.), *Thriving in transitions: A research-based approach to college student success* (pp. 41–64). University of South Carolina, National Resource Center for the First-Year Experience and Students in Transition.

Nelson, L. J., & Barry, C. M. (2005). Distinguishing features of emerging adulthood: The role of self-classification as an adult. *Journal of Adolescent Research, 20*, 242–262.

Nelson, L. J., & Padilla-Walker, L. M. (2013). Flourishing and floundering in emerging adult college students. *Emerging Adulthood, 1*, 67–78. doi:10.1177/2167696812470938

Nelson, L. J., Padilla-Walker, L. M., Carroll, J. S., Madsen, S., Barry, C. M., & Badger, S. (2007). "If you want me to treat you like an adult, start acting like one!" Comparing the criteria that emerging adults and their parents have for adulthood. *Journal of Family Psychology, 21,* 665–674.

Nelson, L. J., Willoughby, B. J., Rogers, A.A., & Padilla-Walker, L. M. (2015). "What a view!": Associations between young people's views of the late teens and twenties and indices of adjustment and maladjustment. *Journal of Adult Development, 22,* 125–137.

Park, M. J., Scott, J. T., Adams, S. H., Brindis, C. D., & Irwin, C. E., Jr. (2014). Adolescent and young adult health in the United States in the past decade: Little improvement and young adults remain worse off than adolescents. *Journal of Adolescent Health, 55,* 3–16. doi:10.1016/j.jadohealth.2014.04.003

Schreiner, L. A. (2012). From surviving to thriving during transitions. In L. A. Schreiner, M. C. Laurie, & D. D. Nelson (Eds.), *Thriving in transitions: A research-based approach to college student success* (pp. 1–18). University of South Carolina, National Resource Center for the First-Year Experience and Students in Transition.

Schreiner, L. A., Louis, M. C., & Nelson, D. D. (Eds.). (2012). *Thriving in transitions: A research-based approach to college student success.* University of South Carolina, National Resource Center for the First-Year Experience and Students in Transition.

Schreiner, L. A., McIntosh, E. J., Nelson, D., & Pothoven, S. (2009). *The thriving quotient: Advancing the assessment of student success.* Paper presented at the Association for the Study of Higher Education, Vancouver, BC.

Schwartz, S. J. (2007). The structure of identity consolidation: Multiple correlated constructs or one superordinate construct? *Identity: An International Journal of Theory and Research, 7,* 27–49.

Schwartz, S. J., Beyers, W., Luyckx, K., Soenens, B., Zamboanga, B. L., Forthun, L. F., . . . Waterman, A. S. (2011). Examining the light and dark sides of emerging adults' identity: A study of identity status differences in positive and negative psychosocial functioning. *Journal of Youth and Adolescence, 40,* 839–859.

Schwartz, S. J., Zamboanga, B. L., Wang, W., & Olthuis, J. V. (2009). Measuring identity from an Eriksonian perspective: Two sides of the same coin? *Journal of Personality Assessment, 91,* 143–154.

Steinberg, L. (2008). A social neuroscience perspective on adolescent risk-taking. *Developmental Review, 28,* 78–106.

Syed, M., & Mitchell, L. L. (2013). Race, identity, and emerging adulthood: Retrospect and prospects. *Emerging Adulthood, 1,* 83–95.

Taber-Thomas, B., & Perez-Edgar, K. (2016). Emerging adulthood brain development. In J. J. Arnett (Ed.), *Handbook of emerging adulthood* (pp. 126–141). Oxford University Press.

U.S. Department of Justice. (2019). Criminal victimization: 2018. https://www.bjs.gov/content/pub/pdf/cv18.pdf.

Waterman, A. S. (2007). Doing well: The relationship of identity status to three conceptions of well-being. *Identity: An International Journal of Theory and Research, 7,* 289–307.

World Health Organization. (2016). Top 10 causes of death. https://www.who.int/gho/mortality_burden_disease/causes_death/top_10/en/

Index

For the benefit of digital users, indexed terms that span two pages (e.g., 52–53) may, on occasion, appear on only one of those pages.

Tables are indicated by *t* following the page number

abbreviations, communication and, 5
academic achievement, impact of technology on, 59–61
academic advising
  implications for retention and success, 97–99
  and student-faculty relationships, 87
acronyms, communication and, 5
activism, and identity development, 17
adjustment trajectories, 16
advising
  implications for retention and success, 97–99
  and student-faculty relationships, 87
affirmation, and cultural group membership, 32
Allison, Kelsie, biography, xi
anxiety, 4
  impact of social media on mental health, 58–59
  prevalence among emerging adults, 22
Arizona State University, First-Year Success Center, 101–5
Arnett, Jeffrey Jensen
  definition of "emerging adulthood," 2
  identity as interpersonal, 10
  optimism among generations, 17
  positive features of emerging adulthood, 117
attachment security, identity development and, 13–14
attachment theory, 39
autonomy
  and development in emerging adults, 114
  and well-being, 39–40
autonomy-supportive parenting, 42
  and absence of parental support, 45–46

case study, 46–47
  collegiate experience, impact of parental involvement, 43–44
  first-generation college students, 44–45
  Guiding Questions, 47–48
Ayers, Kenneth L., biography, xi

Bates, A., social media and identity development, 55–56
bias, and motivational trajectories, 16
Black, Indigenous, and People of Color (BIPOC) students
  parental support, importance of, 44
  peer support, importance of, 46
  social media use and identity development, 56
  transition to campus life, 84
brain development, in emerging adults, 113–14
Brown, G., impact of technology on relationships, 57
Buhl, H. M., attachment security, 13–14
bullying, and impact of social media on mental health, 58–59
Buskirk-Cohen, Allison A., biography, xi

Caillouet, Lindsey (Ellen), biography, xi
campus life
  and experiences with technology, 57–58, 62–63
  promoting relationships campus-wide, 84–85
  and transitions to new relationships, 82–84
career goals, and faculty-student relationships, 89

cell phones, impact on relationships, 57
characteristics of emerging
    adulthood, 2
Chen, P. S. D., impact of technology on
    learning, 60
classroom, limiting technology in, 72
classroom engagement, and faculty-student
    relationships, 87
Cline, F. W., helicopter parenting, 40
coaching
    First-Year Success Center, Arizona State
        University, 101–5
    implications for retention and
        success, 99–101
cocurricular experiences, social media
    and, 73
colearning, and positive identity
    development, 26–29
college socialization, and social
    media, 71–72
collegiate experience
    and absence of parental support, 45–46
    first-generation students, 44–45
    impact of parental involvement
        on, 43–44
    peer support, 46
commitment
    identity development and, 9–10, 32
    and psychosocial functioning, 22–23
communication, 75
    asynchronous vs. synchronous, 70–71
    case study, 75–77
    COVID-19 pandemic, 68
    demographic differences, 70–71
    emojis, 70
    generational differences, 5
    language online, 69–70
    news consumption, modalities
        of, 68–69
    online communication, characteristics and
        strategies, 68–71
    political opinions, using social media to
        express, 69
    social media, effects of, 70
    textisms, 70
communication, adapting to student styles
    and platforms, 71–74
    case study, 75–77
    classroom, limiting technology in, 72
    college socialization, and social
        media, 71–72

electronic access to information, 71
    faculty and student service
        professionals, 72
    learning activities
        preferred frequency of contact, 74
    smartphones, classroom use of, 73
    social and cocurricular experiences, 73
    student affairs professionals, 73–74
community engagement, and identity
    development, 17
competence, and well-being, 39–40
confidence, and student-faculty
    relationships, 88
Cor, Deanna N., biography, xii
Correa, Kevin, biography, xii
COVID-19 pandemic
    communication strategies during, 68
    effects on academic structure, 115
    technology and educational
        opportunities, 60–61
    technology and promoting positive health
        outcomes, 59
cultural context, identity development
    across, 31
cultural identity, development of, 31–33
culture, and identity development, 10–12
cyberbullying, and impact of social media on
    mental health, 58–59

depression, 4
    impact of social media on mental
        health, 58–59
    prevalence among emerging
        adults, 22
development, of emerging adults, 110–12,
    120–21
    autonomy, exercise of, 114
    brain development, 113–14
    education, significant role of, 119–20
    focus on whole person, 113–16, 120
    high-risk behaviors, 114
    identity development, 117
    interdependent domains, 111–12
    leveraging development, 117–19
    optimism and energy, 118–19
    and organizational structure of higher
        education, 114–16
    positive features of emerging
        adulthood, 117
    and promoting student success in higher
        education, 110–12, 114–16

recommendations for higher
education, 121–22
digital divide, 54, 62–63
digital environment, psychological stressors
in, 73–74
digital natives *vs.* digital immigrants, 3
discrimination, and developing self-
efficacy, 14–15
Duncan, Tisha A., biography, xii
Dunn, T. J., technology and academic
achievement, 60

education, and well-being in
adulthood, 119–20
Eichas, Kyle, biography, xii
emerging adulthood
characteristics and challenges, 2
definition of, 2
emojis, and communication preferences, 70
emotional development, 4
anxiety, prevalence among emerging
adults, 22
depression, prevalence among emerging
adults, 22
frameworks for identity
development, 23–25
Guiding Questions, 33
identity and psychosocial
functioning, 22–25
positive identity development, 25–29
positive identity development,
recommendations for
professionals, 29–33
sociocultural context, 30–33
engagement
classroom engagement and faculty-
student relationships, 87
as group process, 26–29
ethnic identity
and positive identity
development, 31–33
and transition to campus life, 84
exploration, identity development and, 9–10,
22–23, 32

faculty
adapting to student communication styles
and platforms, 72
and meaningful relationships with
students, 87–89
and student socialization, 97–98

family, influence and role of, 38
and absence of parental
support, 45–46
case study, 46–47
collegiate experience, impact on,
43–44, 85
developmentally appropriate
parenting, 42–46
family systems theory and adult
attachment, 39
first-generation college
students, 44–45, 84
Guiding Questions, 47–48
helicopter parenting, 40–42
self-determination theory, 39–40
family relationships, 4
family systems theory, 39
Fay, J., helicopter parenting, 40
first-generation college students
coaching programs, 100–1
influence and role of family, 44–45
retention strategies, 96–97
transition to campus life, 84
First-Year Success Center, Arizona State
University, 101–5
Forste, R., social media and academic
achievement, 60

Gee, J. P., online language, 69–70
gender, and communication
preferences, 70–71
ghosting, and impact of technology on
relationships, 57, 62–63

harassment, and impact of social media on
mental health, 58–59
Hayes, E. R., online language, 69–70
health outcomes, technology and promoting
positive, 59
helicopter parenting, 40–42
case study, 46–47
hidden curriculum, first-generation college
students and, 96
higher education
applying research to practices in, 3
future recommendations, 121–22
institutional focus on whole
person, 116
offerings and challenges, 2
organizational structure offered
by, 114–16

identity, and psychosocial
    functioning, 22–25
identity development, 4, 8, 17
    allowing time for, 29
    attachment security, 13–14
    building identity-supportive
        relationships, 29–30
    as central task of emerging adulthood, 117
    creating opportunities for self-
        construction and discovery, 30
    duration of, 10
    exploration vs. commitment, 9–10
    frameworks for, 23–25
    Guiding Questions, 18, 33
    imposter phenomenon, 15–16
    intergroup, 10–12
    interpersonal, 9–10
    interpersonal vs. intergroup, 9
    positive identity development, 25–29
    positive identity development,
        recommendations for
        professionals, 29–33
    self-awareness and, 12–14
    self-efficacy and, 14–16
    self-focus and, 10
    self-motivation and, 16–17
    social identity theory, 8–9
    sociocultural context, 30–33
iGeneration, characteristics and strategies of
    online communication, 69–71
imposter phenomenon, and identity
    development, 15–16
intergroup identity development, 10–12
interpersonal identity development, 9–10
intersectionality, and identity
    development, 10–12

Jacobsen, W. C., social media and academic
    achievement, 60
Junco, R. R., impact of technology on
    learning, 60

Kennedy, J., technology and academic
    achievement, 60

Lane, Joel A., biography, xiii
language.
    characteristics of online, 69–70
    generational differences, 5
learning, impact of technology
    on, 59–61, 72–73

LeFebre, L. E., ghosting, 57
LGBTQ+ students, social media use and
    identity development, 55–56
Life Course Journal, and positive identity
    development, 26–29, 27t
life transitions
    and developing self-efficacy, 15
    and developing self-motivation, 17

Marcia, J. E., identity status model, 23
Martinez Alemán, Ana M.,
    biography, xiii
McCready, Adam M., biography, 13
Meca, Allan
    biography, xiii
    ethnic-racial identity, 33
mental health, impact of technology on, 58–59
mentoring, implications for retention and
    success, 98–99
Miami Adult Development Project, 25–29
    Life Course Journal, 26–29, 27t
    self-construction and self-discovery, 26–27
motivation
    fostering student sense of, 88–89
    identity development and, 16–17

Nelson, Larry J.
    biography, xiv
    motivational trajectories, 16
news consumption, modalities of, 68–69
Nicol, A. A., technology and academic
    achievement, 60

online communication, adapting to student
    styles and platforms, 71–74
    classroom, limiting technology in, 72
    college socialization, and social
        media, 71–72
    electronic access to information, 71
    faculty and student service
        professionals, 72
    learning activities
    preferred frequency of contact, 74
    smartphones, classroom use of, 73
    social and cocurricular experiences, 73
    student affairs professionals, 73–74
online communication, characteristics and
    strategies, 68–71, 75
    asynchronous vs. synchronous
        communication, 70–71
    case study, 75–77

COVID-19 pandemic, 68
demographic differences, 70–71
language online, 69–70
news consumption, modalities of, 68–69
political opinions, using social media to
express, 69
social media, effects of, 70
oppression, and identity
development, 10–12
optimism, of emerging adulthood, 118–19

Padilla-Walker, L. M., motivational
trajectories, 16
parental relationships
significance of, 4, 85
parenting, developmentally appropriate, 43
and absence of parental support, 45–46
case study, 46–47
collegiate experience, impact of parental
involvement, 43–44
first-generation college students, 44–45
Guiding Questions, 47–48
parents, influence and role of, 38
absence of parental support, 45–46
case study, 46–47
collegiate experience, impact on, 43–44
developmentally appropriate
parenting, 42–46
family systems theory and adult
attachment, 39
first-generation college students, 44–45
Guiding Questions, 47–48
helicopter parenting, 40–42
self-determination theory, 39–40
participatory colearning, and positive
identity development, 26–29
peer support
coaching case study, 101–5
coaching programs, 99–101
and collegiate experience, 46, 85–86
First-Year Success Center, Arizona State
University, 101–5
mentoring, 98–99
retention and success, implications
for, 96–97
Phinney, J. S., cultural identity
development, 32
Pitman, R., attachment security, 13
political opinions, using social media to
express, 69
positive identity development, 25–29

Guiding Questions, 33
Life Course Journal, 26–29, 27t
self-construction and self-
discovery, 26–27
positive identity development,
recommendations for
professionals, 29–33
building identity-supportive
relationships, 29–30
creating opportunities for self-
construction and discovery, 30
identity development, allowing time
for, 29
sociocultural context, 30–33
Prensky, M., digital natives vs. digital
immigrants, 3
privilege, and identity development, 10–
12, 16
psychosocial functioning, identity
and, 22–25
purpose, fostering student sense of, 88–89

racial identity
and communication preferences, 70–71
and positive identity development, 31–33
racism
and developing self-efficacy, 14–15
and developing self-motivation, 16
Reed-Fitzke, Kayla, biography, xiv
relatedness, and well-being, 39–40
relationships, building meaningful, 5,
82, 89–90
across institutional boundaries, 84–85
case study, 90–91
Guiding Questions, 91
parent-emerging adult relationships, 85
student-faculty relationships, 87–89
student-peer relationships, 85–86
transitions to new relationships, 82–84
relationships, impact of social media
on, 56–58
retention, challenges for, 5–6
retention, supporting students
in, 5–6, 95–96
advising and mentoring, 97–99
case study, 101–5
coaching, 99–101
First-Year Success Center, Arizona State
University, 101–5
Guiding Questions, 105
hidden curriculum, 96

Rivas-Drake, D., ethnic-racial
identity, 32
Rodil, Julie, biography, xiv
Rowan-Kenyon, Heather T., biography, xiv

Salzano, G., technology and health
outcomes, 59
Scharfe, E., attachment security, 13
Schwartz, S. J., clusters of identity
status, 23–25
self-awareness, identity development
and, 12–14
self-confidence, building through peer
coaching programs, 105
self-construction, and positive identity
development, 26–27
self-determination theory, 39–40
self-discovery, and positive identity
development, 26–27
self-efficacy, identity development
and, 14–16
self-esteem, and student-faculty
relationships, 88
self-focus, identity development and, 10
self-motivation, identity development
and, 16–17
Serna, K. L., frequency of student
contact, 74
smartphones, classroom use of, 73
social capital, and social media, 55
social development, 4
anxiety, prevalence among emerging
adults, 22
depression, prevalence among emerging
adults, 22
frameworks for identity
development, 23–25
Guiding Questions, 33
identity and psychosocial
functioning, 22–25
positive identity development, 25–29
positive identity development,
recommendations for
professionals, 29–33
sociocultural context, 30–33
social experiences, social media
and, 73
social identity theory, 8–9
and social media, 56
socialization, student, 97–98, 104

social media
college socialization and, 71–72
impact on mental health, 58–59
impact on relationships, 56–58
impact on self, 55–56
negative effect on communication
skills, 70
positive effect on social support, 70
social relationships
attachment security and, 13
building meaningful, 5
and self-awareness, 12–13
social support, parental, 85
sociocultural context
identity development and, 30–33
and parental involvement in collegiate
experience, 44
success, supporting students in, 95–96
advising and mentoring, 97–99
case study, 101–5
coaching, 99–101
First-Year Success Center, Arizona State
University, 101–5
Guiding Questions, 105
hidden curriculum, 96
Swanson, Joan A.
biography, xv
technology, 53, 54
Symonds, Sylvia, biography, xv

Tajfel, H., social identity theory, 56
Taylor, Z. W., frequency of student
contact, 74
technology, education and advances of, 3
technology, experiences with, 5, 53, 61
building social capital, 55
and campus life, 57–58
case study, 62–63
digital divide, 54, 62–63
Guiding Questions, 63
impact on learning, 59–61
impact on mental health, 58–59
impact on relationships, 56–58
impact on self, 55–56
online harassment and bullying, 58–59
promoting positive health outcomes, 59
texting, impact on relationships, 56–57
textisms, and communication
preferences, 70
Thuha (Ha) Hoang, biography, xiii

transitions
  and developing self-efficacy, 15
  and developing self-motivation, 17
  and new relationships, 82–84
Turner, J. C., social identity theory, 56

Vannucci, A., technology and mental
  health, 58

Walker, E., technology, 53, 54
Waterman, A. S., identity
  development among college
  students, 23–25
Watters, Elizabeth R.,
  biography, xv

Yarri, Allison, biography, xv